Gender, Food and COVID-19

This book documents how COVID-19 impacts gender, agriculture, and food systems across the globe with on-the-ground accounts and personal reflections from scholars, practitioners, and community members.

During the coronavirus pandemic with many people under lockdown, continual agricultural production and access to food remain essential. Women provide much of the formal and informal work in agriculture and food production, distribution, and preparation often under precarious conditions. A cadre of scholars and practitioners from across the globe provide their timely observations on these issues as well as more personal reflections on its impact on their lives and work. Four major themes emerge from these accounts and are interwoven throughout: the pervasiveness of food insecurity, the ubiquity of women's care work, food justice, and policies and research that can result in a resilience that reimagines the future for greater gender and intersectional equality. We identify what lessons we can learn from this global pandemic about research and practices related to gender, food, and agricultural systems to strive for more equitable arrangements.

This book will be of great interest to students, scholars, and practitioners working on gender and food and agriculture during this global pandemic and beyond.

Paige Castellanos is currently an Assistant Research Professor at Pennsylvania State University, US, in Ag Sciences Global and Rural Sociology. She is the co-editor of the *Routledge Handbook of Gender and Agriculture* (Routledge, 2020).

Carolyn E. Sachs is Professor Emerita of Rural Sociology and Women's, Gender, and Sexuality Studies at Pennsylvania State University, US. She is the co-editor of the *Routledge Handbook of Gender and Agriculture* (Routledge, 2020) and editor of *Gender, Agriculture and Agrarian Transformations* (Routledge, 2019).

Ann R. Tickamyer is Professor Emerita of Rural Sociology and Demography at Pennsylvania State University, US. She is the author and editor of multiple books, including *Rural Poverty in the United States* (2017, with Jennifer Sherman and Jennifer Warlick).

Routledge Focus on Environment and Sustainability

The Ecological Constitution
Reframing Environmental Law
Lynda Collins

Effective Forms of Environmental Diplomacy
Leila Nicolas and Elie Kallab

Coastal Wetlands Restoration
Public Perception and Community Development
Edited by Hiromi Yamashita

Sustainability in High-Excellence Italian Food and Wine
Laura Onofri

Learning to Live with Climate Change
From Anxiety to Transformation
Blanche Verlie

Social Innovation in the Service of Social and Ecological Transformation
The Rise of the Enabling State
Olivier De Schutter and Tom Dedeurwaerdere

Gender, Food and COVID-19
Global Stories of Harm and Hope
Edited by Paige Castellanos, Carolyn E. Sachs and Ann R. Tickamyer

For more information about this series, please visit: www.routledge.com /Routledge-Focus-on-Environment-and-Sustainability/book-series/RFES

Gender, Food and COVID-19

Global Stories of Harm and Hope

**Edited by Paige Castellanos,
Carolyn E. Sachs and
Ann R. Tickamyer**

Routledge
Taylor & Francis Group

LONDON AND NEW YORK

First published 2022
by Routledge
2 Park Square, Milton Park, Abingdon, Oxon OX14 4RN

and by Routledge
605 Third Avenue, New York, NY 10158

Routledge is an imprint of the Taylor & Francis Group, an informa business

© 2022 selection and editorial matter, Paige Castellanos, Carolyn E. Sachs and Ann R. Tickamyer; individual chapters, the contributors

The right of Paige Castellanos, Carolyn E. Sachs and Ann R. Tickamyer to be identified as the authors of the editorial material, and of the authors for their individual chapters, has been asserted in accordance with sections 77 and 78 of the Copyright, Designs and Patents Act 1988.

The Open Access version of this book, available at www.taylorfrancis .com, has been made available under a Creative Commons Attribution-Non Commercial-No Derivatives 4.0 license.

Trademark notice: Product or corporate names may be trademarks or registered trademarks, and are used only for identification and explanation without intent to infringe.

British Library Cataloguing-in-Publication Data
A catalogue record for this book is available from the British Library

Library of Congress Cataloging-in-Publication Data
Names: Castellanos, Paige, editor. | Sachs, Carolyn E., 1950-editor. | Tickamyer, Ann R., editor.
Title: Gender, food and COVID-19: global stories of harm and hope/edited by Paige Castellanos, Carolyn E. Sachs and Ann R. Tickamyer.
Description: Abingdon, Oxon; New York, NY: Routledge, 2022. | Series: Routledge focus on environment and sustainability | Includes bibliographical references and index.
Identifiers: LCCN 2021033490 (print) | LCCN 2021033491 (ebook) | ISBN 9781032055985 (hardback) | ISBN 9781032055992 (paperback) | ISBN 9781003198277 (ebook)
Subjects: LCSH: Women in agriculture. | Food supply. | Agriculture–Social aspects. | COVID-19 (Disease)–Social aspects.
Classification: LCC HD6077 .G446 2022 (print) | LCC HD6077 (ebook) | DDC 338.1082–dc23
LC record available at https://lccn.loc.gov/2021033490
LC ebook record available at https://lccn.loc.gov/2021033491

ISBN: 978-1-032-05598-5 (hbk)
ISBN: 978-1-032-05599-2 (pbk)
ISBN: 978-1-003-19827-7 (ebk)

DOI: 10.4324/9781003198277

Typeset in Times New Roman
by Deanta Global Publishing Services, Chennai, India

Contents

Figures

Contributor biographies

Yuvika Adhikari is currently affiliated to the Southasia Institute of Advanced Studies (SIAS) in Nepal as a Research Officer. Her area of research involves agriculture, migration, and farmer-managed irrigation system in Nepal. Adhikari is a graduate in gender studies from Tribhuwan University.

Robin Becker is a poet and retired professor. Her most recent collection of poems, *The Black Bear Inside Me*, came out in 2018. For 25 years, she taught creative writing at the Pennsylvania State University.

Lia Bryant is a Professor of Sociology at the University of South Australia. She has published extensively on gender and rural society and her books include *Gender and Rurality* (2011, co-authored with Pini, B., Routledge); *Sexuality, Rurality and Geography* (2013 (eds) Gorman-Murray, A., Pini, B., and Bryant, L.); *Women Supervising and Writing Doctoral Theses: Walking on the Grass* (2015, (eds) Bryant, L. and Jaworski, K.); *Critical and Creative Research Methodologies in Social Work* (2015 (ed) Bryant, L., Routledge); and *Water and Rural Communities, Local Meanings, Politics and Place* (2016 with George, J., Routledge).

Hannah Budge is an ESRC-funded PhD researcher at the Centre of Rural Economy, Newcastle University, UK. Her thesis will examine the role of women in agriculture in the Scottish and Canadian Islands, looking at the barriers, in what was traditionally viewed as a masculine industry, experienced between and within these communities. She is interested in how gender impacts on everyday life in rural areas.

Angie Carter lives on 1842 Treaty lands in Michigan's Upper Peninsula. She is a Women, Food and Agriculture Network Board member,

member of the Western UP Food Systems Collaborative, and works as an assistant professor and rural sociologist at Michigan Technological University. Her writing and research study questions of food, land, agriculture, and justice.

Paige Castellanos is an Assistant Research Professor in Ag Sciences Global and Rural Sociology at the Pennsylvania State University, and Program Manager for the Gender Equity through Agricultural Research and Education (GEARE) Initiative. Her research focuses on gender and development and she is a co-editor of the *Routledge Handbook of Gender and Agriculture* (2020).

María del Rosario Castro Bernardini is a researcher in Livelihoods and Rights at Oxfam America. She supports the research production and initiatives of the Women's Economic Rights, Gender Justice & Inclusion Hub and the Food System Department. She co-authored the report "Caring under COVID-19" that was launched as part of the #HowICare campaign. Her research examines the intersection of gender, (unpaid and paid) labor, food systems, and the family. She obtained a dual-title PhD in Rural Sociology and Women's Studies. Originally from Lima, Rosario worked in applied and academic research projects on women's rights, extractive industries, public education, and bureaucratic barriers in Peru.

Afrina Choudhury works as Research Fellow (Senior Gender Specialist) for WorldFish, Bangladesh, where she is responsible for the design and implementation of pro-poor gender-responsive strategies. Working in the field of aquatic-agriculture, her research has revolved around the integration of gender into technical interventions in ways that are sustainable and transformative. She also co-created and chairs the Bangladesh National Gender Working Group, which brings together gender and equity work in Bangladesh.

Marc J. Cohen is Senior Researcher at Oxfam America, currently working on aid effectiveness and global food security. He received his PhD in political science from the University of Wisconsin-Madison. Before joining Oxfam, Marc was a Research Fellow at the International Food Policy Research Institute (IFPRI) from 1998 to 2008. He has carried out field research in Ethiopia, Haiti, Rwanda, Taiwan, Thailand, Uganda, and the US. Marc has taught at American, George Washington, and Johns Hopkins Universities, as well as at the Washington Center for Internships and Academic Seminars and the Universities of Florence and Oslo.

Mercedes García is a member of AMIR and has played an essential leadership role in the organization. Currently she works as the administrative coordinator for AMIR and is one of the members leading the COVID-19 response team supporting the communities.

Phạm Thị Hòa works at the Lam Dong Crop Production and Plant Protection Sub-department. She is responsible for doing forest health surveillance, collecting data and samples, as well as identifying nematodes and fungi causing forest disease in Lam Dong province. She has a PhD in plant pathology from the Zhejiang University in China. Her current research explores the adaptation strategies of flower and vegetable growers in Lam Dong province in the COVID-19 pandemic.

Michaela Hoffelmeyer is a PhD student at the Pennsylvania State University earning a dual-title in Rural Sociology and Women's, Gender, and Sexuality Studies. Her research interests include gender and sexuality in agriculture, sustainability, and food justice. Michaela's research works to understand how social location and power in the agrifood system have implications for rural livelihoods and community vitality.

Sovanneary Huot is a PhD student in Rural Sociology at the Pennsylvania State University. Her work focuses on gender, international agriculture, and community development. Her Master's thesis examined barriers that women farmers in Cambodia face in acquiring and working in leadership positions. Her dissertation will explore the gendered aspects of wild food plant knowledge, use, production, and marketing.

Leif Jensen is Distinguished Professor of Rural Sociology and Demography at the Pennsylvania State University. His research is found within social stratification, demography, and the sociology of economic change, all with an emphasis on rural people and places both in the US and internationally.

Nozomi Kawarazuka is Scientist at the International Potato Center, based in Hanoi, Vietnam. Her research focuses on political economy and political ecology from gender perspectives, exploring the processes of marginalization and exclusion in formal and informal food systems. She is involved in a wide range of interdisciplinary agricultural research such as understanding the adoption of agricultural technologies, the gendered impacts of labour migration on farming practices, and rural youth and ethnic minorities in mountain regions in South and Southeast Asia.

Stephanie Leder is a researcher at the Swedish University of Agricultural Sciences (SLU). She leads a four-year FORMAS-funded project on "Revitalizing community-managed irrigation systems in the context of out-migration in Nepal." Stephanie was a Postdoctoral Fellow at the International Water Management Institute (IWMI) in Nepal, and the CGIAR Program "Water, Land and Ecosystems." Stephanie holds a PhD in Human Geography from the University of Cologne, Germany.

Cynthia McDougall is a Senior Research Fellow at the Stockholm Environment Institute (SEI). She is an interdisciplinary social scientist with over 20 years of experience in food security, gender and social equity, and natural resource governance. Cynthia holds a Master's degree in Geography from Cambridge University, and a PhD in Knowledge, Technology and Innovation from Wageningen University.

Olga Pérez is AMIR's project coordinator. She has played an important role in the search, development, and implementation of new projects for AMIR. Currently she is leading the COVID-19 response team to support the communities.

Surendran Rajaratnam is a Postdoctoral Fellow at WorldFish, Malaysia. He is currently working to integrate gender into technical aquaculture and small-scale fisheries work with the Government of Assam, India, as part of the Assam Agribusiness and Rural Transformation Project. He also conducts studies on women's self-help groups in the fisheries and aquaculture in India. Surendran serves the GAF Section of the Asian Fisheries Society as an Executive Committee member and the editor of the section's newsletter. Surendran holds a Master's degree and a PhD in Social Work from Universiti Sains Malaysia.

Alfredo Reyes is a PhD student in Rural Sociology and International Agriculture and Development at Penn State University. His research interests are found in three broad areas: international rural social change, international migration, and international development with specific interest in the intersection of gender, agriculture, and the diffusion of innovations.

Whitney Shervey holds an MS in Food Systems and Society from Oregon Health and Science University and is currently the Food Program Coordinator at a nonprofit healthcare and social services agency. Her 20 years of experience as a professional cook inspire her research on labor organizing in the foodservice industry at the intersection of gender, race, and class.

Sally Shortall is the Duke of Northumberland Chair of Rural Economy, in Newcastle University. She is well known for her research in the field of rural social science generally and is specifically known for her work on gender and agriculture. Sally Shortall was twice elected President of the European Society for Rural Sociology (2015–2017; 2017–2019). She was elected First Vice-President of the International Rural Sociology Association (2016–2020) and is currently President-Elect of the International Rural Sociology Association. Sally was recently elected a Fellow of the Academic of Social Sciences.

Gitta Shrestha works as a researcher at the International Water Management Institute. She has training in geography, human geography, and in the study of human adaptation to natural resource constraints in India, Nepal, and Europe. Her research interest involves inquiring into the reproduction of social and gender inequalities and its impact on changing human–environment relations.

Emily M. L. Southard is a graduate student of Rural Sociology at the Pennsylvania State University. She is interested in all topics of (in)justice in the agro-food system. Her research focuses primarily on gender issues in peasant communities, migration, and labor patterns related to gender and agriculture, and gendered effects of climate change on rural livelihoods.

Ann R. Tickamyer is Emerita Professor of Rural Sociology and Demography with affiliations in Sociology and Gender and Women's Studies at Penn State University. Her scholarship centers on rural poverty, gender, development, and livelihood practices, and their relationship to disaster and climate change in the US and in Southeast Asia.

Rachana Upadhyaya is a researcher at the Southasia Institute of Advanced Studies (SIAS) in Nepal. She holds an Erasmus Mundus Double Master's Degree in Gender and Women's Studies from University of Hull, UK, and University of Lodz, Poland. She has more than ten years' experience of working on gender issues in Nepal, both in academia and practice. The principal focus of her work at present is studying urban risk and resilience through an intersectional perspective.

Hazel Velasco is a graduate student in Rural Sociology and International Agriculture and Development at Penn State University. Her interests are found broadly in the sociology of international rural social change and the determinants of effective collective action, with special attention on the intersection of gender and indigenous communities in Latin America.

Kayla Yurco is an Assistant Professor of Geographic Science in the School of Integrated Sciences at James Madison University. She is a graduate of the Pennsylvania State University (PhD, Geography) and the University of Michigan (MS, Natural Resources and Environment) and a former Graduate Fellow of the International Livestock Research Institute (ILRI) in Nairobi, Kenya. Her research and teaching center on the intersection of gender, environment, and development.

Acknowledgments

We would like to thank all of the people who wrote for the blog on Gender, Food, Agriculture and Coronavirus. We wish we could have published all of the blogs, but for the purposes of having a short book that was published in a timely fashion, we could only choose a small selection of authors. We would also like to express our gratitude for the chapter authors in this book, who wrote their chapters in record time. We received support for the blog and the book from the Penn State College of Agricultural Sciences Office of Research and Graduate Education and the Horace T. Woodward Faculty Development Fund, Penn State Ag Sciences Global, and Penn State Department of Agricultural Economics, Sociology and Education. Without the support of Deanna Behring and Laszlo Kulcsar, we would not have been able to make the online version of the book freely available. Thanks goes to our editor, Hannah Ferguson, for encouraging us to move forward with this book as well as John Baddeley for all of his attention to detail. Special love to Armando and Madeleine Castellanos who supported our efforts and did their own share of care work for new baby Xavier during many meetings and work sessions for the book and blog. Finally, we would like to acknowledge all of the people who have struggled, died, and cared for people due to COVID-19 and especially the women who have led the charge to help others, as healthcare workers, teachers, community leaders and activists, farmers, food system workers, mothers, and in many other roles, during this difficult time for people across the globe.

Introduction

Paige Castellanos, Carolyn E. Sachs, and Ann R. Tickamyer

Underlying conditions

> While we were not looking, they increased
> the number of Birds per Minute (BPM)
> at the poultry processing plant. When line
>
> speeds increase, accidents increase, two
> feet apart isn't six, the USDA
> goes along, squeezing workers together
>
> as the National Chicken Council dictates.
> The underlying condition of poultry
> Workers is *murder by design*. Ask the woman—
>
> blue, cold—handling eviscerated carcasses
> > on the refrigeration side.

This poem by Robin Becker, originally contributed to our blog on "Gender, Food, Agriculture, and the Coronavirus" (www.sites.psu.edu /geareblog) in the first year of the pandemic, conveys some of the horror and hardship brought about by COVID-19 in its initial stages. Food shortages, disruptions in agricultural and food production, processing, and distribution, and illness among workers struggling to provide essential services under extreme conditions were among the first evidence of the devastation that would ensue over the next year and a half and counting. As news spread of pandemic effects, we decided to add our voices to the effort to document and understand what COVID-19 has meant for the nexus of gender, food, and agriculture across the globe. Inspired by the blog and recognizing how intertwined individual stories are with larger social and structural processes, we want this account to be both scholarly and personal, to tell our stories and link them to collective welfare and action.

The coronavirus pandemic upended our world and almost every aspect of our lives. The year 2020 was marked by social distancing and mask wearing, but more profoundly by an overwhelming burden – of patients on healthcare systems stretched thin, of grief from the loss of loved ones, of economies crippled by prevention measures, and of the need to juggle work and family responsibilities. Threatening every corner of the world, the pandemic's widespread impact will likely have repercussions for many years to come. By December of 2021, although signs of hope have emerged with the rollout of multiple vaccines and deepening understanding of how the disease operates, its devastation is far from over. With over 265 million cases, more than 5.2 million deaths worldwide, and new surges and variants, the need for vigilance remains critical. Especially as evidence of the extent of disparities in vulnerabilities, risks, and outcomes for different populations has grown, the need to document and witness these impacts has also increased. We know about differential mortality and morbidity by gender, age, race, ethnicity, and social class. We know that poverty of persons and places increases risk, vulnerability, and effective response. We know the types and extent of burdens experienced differ by these same factors. And we know these disparities manifest in basic survival and livelihood practices. Women's and men's encounters with the disease vary dramatically. Men are more likely to die and yet less willing to protect themselves with vaccination. Women face more vulnerability to job loss and assume a higher burden of home and care work. The fallout from these and many other differences are only now beginning to be manifested, analyzed, and understood with the end of the pandemic not yet in sight.

As the pandemic spread in early 2020, we realized the likelihood of a widespread gendered impact and the importance of developing a timely global exchange about COVID-19, gender, food, and agriculture. Beginning with an epilogue in the edited book *Gender and Agriculture Handbook* (Sachs et al. 2020), we solicited contributions from authors about the initial impacts of the pandemic on gender and agriculture in their regions or topics. The overwhelming response, on short notice, highlighted the critical nature of the nexus of gender, agriculture, and COVID-19. We began our blog to document the challenges faced in the global food system with a gender lens. Contributions detail rich accounts of hardships experienced by rural women and marginalized groups in many parts of the world. As we posted entries, we realize the need to continue to monitor the situation around the world and to deepen our understanding of the gendered disparities in different contexts. We asked a selection of contributors to broaden their entries to include ongoing reflections and to expand the information initially shared in their blog posts. This book is the result.

Across the world, devastating illness, lockdowns, and layoffs in response to the pandemic; the endangered food supply threatens damage to livelihoods, health, and safety. Gender pervades every aspect of food and agriculture systems as food moves from field to table. The role that women play in providing much of the formal and informal work in agriculture, food production, distribution, and preparation became that much more critical. Their ability to perform this work with fair compensation is often framed by inequitable policies and institutions.

Whether managing to care for a baby while continuing work, teaching young children as they remote learn, or supporting elderly parents while separated because of lockdown barriers, many women like us are burdened with unequal care work responsibilities both at home and in their communities. We already know that women have higher rates of care work at home, whether food preparation or childcare, fetching water or fuel, but through the pandemic many have added responsibilities. Women across many different countries and contexts are responsible for the care of multi-generational households, household members who may have returned from migration, and children whose schools are closed. Women also provide much of the formal and informal care work in hospitals, nursing homes, and their households, critical during health care crises but also exposing them to disease.

While many of us are fortunate enough to have comfortable and safe shelter, expansive outdoor spaces to exercise or alleviate stress, and friends, families, and colleagues just a remote video call away, we are still struggling with isolation and worry about overcoming the barriers the pandemic presents in conducting our own work. Others are not as fortunate as illness, homelessness, unemployment, and hunger have become widespread. The nature of this health crisis brings some of the most severe and far-reaching lockdowns the world has known which results in saving lives but, simultaneously, economic disaster as economies plummet. We see mental health concerns rise and increases in domestic violence across the globe. We know that in a range of crises such as earthquakes, droughts, hurricanes, floods, and health pandemics, intersectional inequalities often result in devasting consequences particularly for the poor, minorities, and women. The economic consequences typically exacerbate existing inequalities, create new ones, and have the highest impact on the poor and marginalized populations, resulting in increasing malnutrition and food insecurity. Despite their vulnerability, women are not mere victims. We know that individual women and women's groups and organizations show remarkable resilience during periods of crisis. During the pandemic, women's groups are creating just and sustainable initiatives of care and working to make this crisis an opportunity for systemic change from the local to the global level.

This book presents cases from across the world to document how COVID-19 impacts gender, agriculture, and food systems across the globe with on-the-ground accounts from scholars, practitioners, and community members. We organize the accounts around four emergent themes: food insecurity, care work, intersectional inequalities, and moving beyond COVID-19 in research and policy. Intertwined are recurring threads about hunger, precarity, and safety. We conclude with policies that reimagine the future for greater gender and intersectional equality.

Food insecurity

The continuing global health pandemic results in increased food insecurity, especially for already vulnerable populations. As people lose their jobs and sources of income, they often lack resources to purchase or produce adequately nutritious food. With lockdowns, small farmers, many of whom are women, often struggle to transport or market their agricultural produce. Other women farmers and vendors in some parts of the world saw the demand for their local food escalate as a result of some of the lockdowns and safety fears of going to large markets.

Leder et al.'s chapter examines the case of Nepal, highlighting the challenges to food security for women farmers and the issues related to the government response. Because of the shutdowns from the pandemic, many women farmers were unable to sell their harvest or were selling at a much lower price, experiencing food waste, and struggling to make their expected living. Left out of the government response, women farmers manage their and their families' food insecurity with little assistance, relying on their own social networks for support. Huot and Jensen's chapter details the impacts of COVID-19 on women in Cambodia. They expand the discussion beyond issues of food security to related issues due to school closures, tourism shutdowns, and return migration. In Kawarazuka and Hoa's chapter, as the market dropped out, women were able to find strength in their own skills and teams. Agribusiness entrepreneurs faced severe challenges in Vietnam due to lack of tourism; however, they have managed to capitalize on their experience and through their existing networks have made efforts not only to survive but to thrive during the difficult economic times. Throughout this section, a common theme is the role and reach of government response, whether through direct food or economic aid or in restrictions that prevent the spread of the virus but negatively impact economic and market activities. In each case, women and men experience these hardships differently, whether it is the increased carework burden, the challenges to access aid benefits, or the difficulty in maintaining food security. However, this section on food insecurity demonstrates that when given certain opportunities and assets, women develop their own networks and find ways to mitigate the challenges.

Carework in families, households, and communities

Women often provide the bulk of food care work for their families, households, and communities. This largely unpaid work has been taken for granted and undervalued. The pandemic increased women's household food care work as people spend more time working at home and children are not in school in many places. In addition to providing the bulk of care work in their homes, women are often at the forefront of leading innovative community care initiatives.

Budge and Shortall describe the additional burdens of domestic labor that the pandemic has imposed on farm women in Scotland and the inequalities these have generated and exacerbated. They argue that research on inequalities in the gendered divisions of labor must include more work on intra-household responsibilities, including mental labor. Yurco elaborates on the importance of care work in multiple forms and contexts during the pandemic, including among pastoralists in Kenya and in her own backyard. She too argues that it pervades every aspect of life during the pandemic, and more thought and effort must be given to the topic in its aftermath.

Intersectional inequalities in the food system

This section focuses on strategies for overcoming overlapping racial, gender, ethnic, sexuality, and class inequalities. Food injustice, which exists in ordinary times, becomes more problematic in the extraordinary circumstances created by the pandemic. This entire volume represents intersectional analysis of gender with other social locations within food and agricultural systems, while the chapters in this section document specific intersectional vulnerabilities, coping mechanisms, and resilience for marginalized populations in the United States and Central America.

In their chapter, Reyes, Velasco, Garcia, and Perez show how indigenous farming women in Honduras struggled to get their crops to market during pandemic lockdowns. Garcia and Perez, who are involved in a local women's organization, show how the organization quickly adapted their efforts in the pandemic to provide sanitation, masks, and food to women members. Carter also works with a women's NGO, Women's Food and Agricultural Network (WFAN), from her home in Minnesota. The pandemic occurred simultaneously with the brutal police killing of George Floyd, a black man, in Minneapolis. WFAN responded to both, providing online social support and information to women farmers and initiating discussions about race and racism in agriculture. She discusses similar work with a local organization of Ojibiwe people and white settlers that provided food assistance during the pandemic and discussed racism in the food system and in their community. In her chapter on migrant farm and food-processing workers in the United States, Southard shows how the intersectionality of race, ethnicity, citizenship, and gender shapes the powerlessness of these workers. As she reveals, during the pandemic they are essential for providing food for everyone, but are treated as disposable. Hoffelmyer discusses how queer people throughout the food system, as farmworkers, farmers, restaurant workers, meat-processing workers, and consumers, have been impacted by the pandemic. She documents how one queer-owned farm in rural New York mobilized during the pandemic to meet the needs of queer farmers and consumers, especially people of color. Shervey discusses how restaurant workers, many of whom are women of color, have been hard-hit by structural racism and the impact of COVID-19. Many lost their jobs, while others risk their lives as they go to work to earn income and provide food for others. She delves into the efforts of restaurant workers to organize during COVID-19 both for better working conditions and to address racism in the food industry.

Beyond COVID-19: moving forward with research and policy

The section highlights the challenges of conducting research during the pandemic and the policies and programs that have emerged as a consequence. The pandemic demonstrates the pervasiveness of inequalities and injustice in food and agricultural systems both globally and locally that play out in forms of insecurity, precarity, and scarcity for producers, workers, and consumers alike. In addition to documenting these impacts, contributors to this volume note necessary policies and practices that could make a difference now and, especially, moving forward once the pandemic ends. "Beyond COVID-19" includes accounts of how accepted research practices need to change to accommodate the realities of attempting to collect necessary data during pandemic restrictions and how this informs better policy. Tickamyer discusses the impacts of COVID-19 on research programs around the globe and how these reinforce the urgency of using feminist methodology and participatory approaches to maintain access, respect boundaries, and advance understanding within ethical standards when options are limited. Choudhury, Rajaratnam, and McDougall urge for more sex-desaggregated data that demonstrate differences between men and women. They highlight women's often unrecognized work in fisheries in Southeast Asia and how, during the pandemic, it was critical to include gender analyses to ensure policy reaches and benefits women. Bryant's meditation on memory and auto-ethnography demonstrates how to unpack meaning when data collection options are restricted in rural Australia. Nkengla, Cohen, and Castro discuss how the global health pandemic became a global food crisis and its ramifications in sub-Saharan Africa. They explain how the pandemic exposed the weaknesses and vulnerabilities of our food systems and suggest policies and strategies for building more just, resilient, and sustainable food systems. Taken together, these chapters offer a blueprint for meaningful change.

Our stories

Moving between the personal and the professional, many of the authors of these accounts also describe their own circumstances while taking stock of the pandemic. We add our stories as testament to our embrace of the prescriptions of feminist methodology – to provide situated knowledge and practice the reflexivity we advocate.

Paige

During the pandemic, I have worked from home, supported a remote learning elementary school child, and welcomed a new baby. Despite the challenges, I recognize how fortunate we are in so many ways – to have flexibility in my job, to have work, to have good healthcare including vaccinations, and to be with my partner as a team. We try to keep a positive outlook, appreciating the extra family time and finding new ways to engage in our community.

Carolyn

I retired a few years ago, but remain involved in a few projects with plans to travel to Honduras and Australia to work on those projects, but I have not ventured far from Pennsylvania. I am privileged to live in the country so I can easily be outdoors. I live alone but am usually a very social person with many people coming into my home. During this year, I improvised by getting an outdoor heater and sat on my deck with friends throughout the year even in the freezing cold weather, so that I would not be lonely. My new puppy also lifts my spirits. Luckily, I don't have to spend the hours on zoom teaching and meeting that my working colleagues are enduring and now that I have had two vaccinations, I feel amazed how wonderful I feel to be with friends and family in person. I hope the same for all people across the world.

Ann

I retired in January 2020 with plans to remain active in ongoing projects but have time to travel and pursue other interests. I returned from research in Alaska as the realities of COVID-19 became obvious and almost immediately went into lockdown. I am lucky: I live where outdoor activities are easy with a husband and dog for companionship; family and friends with broadband for support; vaccinations available; and research projects to allay boredom and provide purpose. I struggle to disentangle the changes and challenges of retirement from those posed by pandemic realities but know that we are among the most fortunate – thus responsible for ensuring that those with less access and agency are heard.

Reference

Sachs, C. E., Jensen, L., Castellanos, P., & Sexsmith, K. (Eds.). (2021). *Routledge handbook of gender and agriculture*. Routledge.

Part 1
Food insecurity

1 COVID-19, gender, and small-scale farming in Nepal

Stephanie Leder, Gitta Shrestha, Rachana Upadhyaya, and Yuvika Adhikari

Introduction: gender and small-scale farming in Nepal in the context of COVID-19

The COVID-19 pandemic, as in most other major socioeconomic crises, affects the health and food security of marginalized populations the most. Social and economic inequalities become visible because households' and communities' responses rely on their existing financial resources, social networks, and reliable information.

In rural Nepal, the most marginalized farmers had limited access to health care facilities, quick financial support, food, and relief measures during COVID-19. For households where everyday food needs are covered through daily wage labor or remittances from out-migrated family members, a pandemic has direct health and food security consequences (Egger et al., 2021). Harmful impacts are immediate income loss, restricted mobility for migrants, and the disruption of food production and market supply chains. However, as Agarwal (2021) argues, COVID-19 not only affects earnings and food insecurity, but also intra-household dynamics and gendered vulnerabilities such as the depletion of savings and assets, social isolation, and mobility loss.

This chapter addresses the impact of COVID-19 lockdown on women farmers, with a particular focus on our field sites in the Far-Western region of Nepal. We review Nepal's government response to COVID-19 with regard to the exclusionary effects of relief and recovery measures for women smallholders. In this context, we highlight the importance of local women's organizations and inclusive (digital) platforms to create awareness of the needs of the most marginalized, and how to effectively reach out to them. Finally, we conclude with recommendations for future research in a post-COVID-19 context.

DOI: 10.4324/9781003198277-2

COVID-19 impacts on women farmers

Access to resources and social networks is gendered, reducing women's resilience to the impacts of pandemics and disasters. Social and gender discriminatory norms within households impact women's health and well-being negatively in rural Nepal. Eating last in the family and dropping first from education falls on women and girls during emergencies. Ensuring water, sanitation, and hygiene is traditionally women's responsibility, and has received greater attention from national and international governments in the recent pandemic. With reduced food security, income, and mobility and increased water stress, girls and women may be forced to compromise on food, health, education, and decision-making. The consequences are evident with a 200 percent increase in the maternal mortality rate when the lockdown began (Poudel, 2020), and increased cases of domestic and sexual violence (Sharma, 2020).

In Nepal, citizens were instructed to maintain physical distancing, which limited their ability to farm, with lockdown beginning March 24, 2020. The supply of agricultural inputs such as seeds and fertilizers was interrupted, and farmers suffered a huge loss since they were unable to transport their products to market. Female smallholder vegetable farmers were hardest hit since they carry and sell vegetables door to door. Many lost their main source of income. In the Dhading district, which supplies a third of vegetables in the capital Kathmandu, vegetables were reported to be "rotting in farms" as mobility restrictions prevented transport to the markets (Adhikari, 2020). The precarity of small-scale farmers' situations during the COVID-19 lockdown was confirmed by a member of a rural women farmers group in Rautahat and Sarlahi in an online meeting of the Gender in Humanitarian Action Task Team conducted by UN Women on April 27, 2020. She reported the risk of growing food insecurity and anxiety of debt return, especially among female-headed households. Women in particular depend on informal loans with high interest rates. The temporary loss of income adds to their vulnerabilities.

We conducted three phone interviews on April 15, 2021, with research participants in our field sites who confirmed similar experiences in Western Nepal. Three residents in the villages of Selinge in the district of Dadeldhura (Ajayameru Municipality) (Figure 1.1), and Tiltali, in the district of Doti (Shikhar municipality), stated that, in their villages, most keep physical distance and stayed at home as advised on the radio and national TV news. They hoped that returning migrants would follow quarantine rules so that the virus would not spread. Limited access to markets severely affected the whole cropping season as they could not purchase agricultural inputs or sell their produce. The supply of soaps, vegetables, or cell-phone recharge cards

Figure 1.1 Mustard on rice terraces in the village Selinge, Dadeldhura, Nepal, in February 2020 shortly before the lockdown (Stephanie Leder).

from the market was limited, as residents were advised not to leave their village, which was perceived as being considerably safe. Instead, a private truck regularly delivered food to them, although limited to those who could afford to buy food. This was problematic for those with limited financial resources if regular remittances no longer arrived.

When we carried out fieldwork again in February 2021 across different villages in the same district, we conducted interviews both with farmers and local government stakeholders. The farmers recounted their stories of agricultural loss during the three months of lockdown. A female commercial vegetable farmer in the village Puilekh in Dadeldhura mentioned "last year the chilies that sold for 120 rupees [NPR, equals to about 1 USD], during lockdown they sold for only 20 rupees [NPR, equals to about 0.17 USD]." Farmers sold their chili for less than one-fifth of the normal market price during COVID-19. Further research is needed to systematically collect data on other vegetable prices across diverse districts.

Similarly, a couple of prominent farmers from the same village shared how COVID-19 mobility restrictions forced them to sell their vegetables and livestock at lower prices in their own village instead of at the local marketplace in Dadeldhura. "What remained after household consumption, we distributed to the neighbors," the wife said. Furthermore, they suffered a loss of approximately 80,000 NPR (equal to about 700 USD) for selling their poultry at lower prices.

We suspect that the short-term food security effects of the lockdown measures were cushioned through the subsistence farming widely prevalent among Nepal's poorest small-scale farmers, and the sharing of surplus produce with neighbors. Further investigations are needed to determine the different effects of the lockdown on households with diverse degrees of involvement in agriculture and different landholding sizes. Of particular importance is the need to assess whether landless laborers' households were supported through local social networks, as they must have faced food shortages while being dependent on daily wages not available during the lockdown. In an earlier study on women's empowerment in water security programs in the same sites in Western Nepal, Leder et al. (2017) found that differences between women, such as age, marital status, caste, remittance flow, and land ownership, led to some benefiting more than others from water and food security programs. Hence, we assume that the poorest and most disadvantaged women are also those most affected by the lockdown, due to their differential access to resources. The study also identified the importance of inter-household relations within communities, as well as intra-household relations: these social relationships strongly shaped women's agency in their ability to secure water and food. We further assume that collective action is an underrecognized factor contributing to household food security in times of restricted mobility and market lockdown, as farmer collectives are able to improve smallholder's food security through the pooling of labor, land, produce, and capital (Leder et al., 2019; Sugden et al., 2020).

Government of Nepal's response for relief and recovery

Shortly after the Government of Nepal imposed a national lockdown, the Council of Ministers, through a decision made on 29 March, directed local governments to arrange vehicles to transport local produce to nearby markets and to the Kathmandu valley. In the same decision, local governments were directed to provide mobility passes for the vehicles of local entrepreneurs transporting local produce to markets.

In May 2020, the Government of Nepal introduced emergency relief packages for farmers. However, voices from the field share the exclusionary consequences of such packages. Certain criteria must be fulfilled in order to be eligible for benefit from the relief, such as land entitlement and land size. The central government has announced a relief package of 750

Nepali rupees (6.20 USD) per kattha (338m²) of land. In Province 2, the government has announced a relief package for farmers who own 10 kattha (3380m²) of land, and cultivate it themselves, to receive 10,000 NPR cash in their accounts. This de facto excludes smallholders, tenant farmers, sharecroppers, and daily agricultural wage laborers, of which the majority are women (Figures 1.2 and 1.3).

This has huge implications on women's well-being and family food security. While men equally suffer psychological stress due to the loss of income in emergencies, women are the ones to sell their assets first, causing increased incidences of poverty among women and women-headed households. Gender scholars repeatedly highlight the imperatives of gender and social inclusion measures in long-term agricultural and food security planning in Nepal. As a study on gendered practices in the water sector in Nepal shows, gender equality and social inclusion attempts only focus on gender quotas of 33 percent of women in water-user associations, without strategies to pursue more inclusive decision-making to overcome unequal and gendered power relations (Shrestha & Clement, 2019).

Figure 1.2 A woman farmer in front of her self-built polyhouse in the village Tiltali, Doti, Nepal, in February 2020 shortly before the corona lockdown. Self-built polyhouses as affordable support from local government (Stephanie Leder).

Figure 1.3 A female wage laborer carrying sand to build a new irrigation pond in the village Syauke, Dadeldhura, Nepal, in February 2020 shortly before the corona lockdown (Stephanie Leder).

Finally, the Government of Nepal and the World Bank signed an 80 million USD agreement to strengthen rural market linkages and promote agricultural entrepreneurship to facilitate post-COVID-19 recovery. The Rural Enterprise and Economic Development (REED) project will be implemented in five economic corridors spanning the seven provinces. The project will use a "cash for work" approach (GoN and WB, 2020). Cash for work is a labor-intensive approach and hence it is important to consider how it can be made gender-responsive, given that women are already overburdened with work due to high care responsibilities and often out-migrated husbands. Furthermore, as the project focuses on market and entrepreneurship, the degree to which it will benefit smallholder subsistence farming groups in order to lessen the risk of food insecurity seems unclear. As our research has demonstrated, local social networks, subsistence farming, and neighborhood sharing were particularly important to ensure food security.

The government of our field study (Province 7, Sudurpaschim) encouraged youth migrant returnees toward agriculture through facilitation and prize-distribution programs targeted toward people who have contributed in the local production through their entrepreneurship. They launched an agriculture subsidy program targeting returnee migrant workers in a bid to control remigration of young men during the pandemic to India or elsewhere. The 150 million NPR program (about 1.3 million USD) was targeted to provide 100,000 to 500,000 NPR (about 860–4300 USD) to more than 5000 workers; however, the number of applicants for the fund exceeded 80,000 (Shah, 2020). In Ajayameru municipality, 500 people applied for the agriculture subsidy and half of them received it. It is hoped that these loans will be used as intended, to support migrants in vegetable farming as well as livestock entrepreneurship such as buffalo and poultry farming, and pig and goat keeping at home. Notably, there will be gendered implications of these loans, as return migrants are predominantly men.

Women's organizations and inclusive digital platforms to spread awareness

Local women leaders and farmer-managed organizations such as water-user associations are important backbones to handle the COVID-19 crisis, as they can reach out to rural farming populations. However, they do not have sufficient resources and influence on decision-making. A webinar organized by the IRDR Centre for Gender and Disaster co-hosted by Pallavi Payal, an independent researcher from Nepal, aimed to explore the lived experiences of women political leaders in Nepal in the time of COVID-19 (Yadav & Payal, 2020). In the webinar, Female Deputy Mayors from Nepal Province 2 said women farmers feel comfortable sharing their concerns with them as female deputy mayors, but they themselves are under- resourced and do not have sufficient influence to make sure relief packages at the district level reach the most marginalized. This shows that local women leaders are approached by women farmers directly about their specific needs during the pandemic, but the mayors themselves are unable to respond to their needs due to their limited financial and human resources.

To address these imbalances, substantial financial support for public awareness campaigns and the supply of relief packages and testing and medical kits via local networks to the most marginalized communities is necessary. Local groups and female health care workers such as Nepal's network of Female Community Health Volunteers may be key informants for marginalized communities and local governments alike. The financial support of local organizations is important as physical distancing is still a prevalent practice to discriminate historically lower-caste members, and social stigma may easily spread and affect returning migrants. Therefore, access to reliable information on precautions and medical measures is needed, building on existing structures at the local level.

Local agriculture cooperatives can be highly responsive to the needs of women farmers. Restricted mobility due to gender norms and care responsibilities cause women farmers to seek agriculture input services closer to home. In Kulche Besi, one of the vegetable pocket areas of Nepal's centrally located Province 3, we conducted a focus group discussion with eight women farmers in January 2021. Women farmers reported food losses due to restricted mobility during the first two months of the lockdown. In Kulche Besi, some smallholders ploughed their fields with ripe tomatoes since they could not sell them due to the lockdown. Women smallholders stressed that vegetable farming would not have been possible during the lockdown without the local agriculture cooperative. The local agriculture cooperative supplied seeds and fertilizers to member farmers during the lockdown when individual mobility was restricted. It also distributed masks to its members which ensured that labor sharing, locally known as "parma," continued during lockdown while avoiding the spread of infection. The agriculture cooperative has a women farmers subcommittee that works with local NGOs such as the Center for Environmental and Agricultural Policy Research, Extension and Development (CEEAPRED), which trains women farmers on the use of organic pesticides and fertilizers. The training on locally resourced organic fertilizers came in handy when there was a scarcity of chemical fertilizer nationally due to the restriction on international imports. This was particularly useful for smallholders and subsistence farmers as locally produced organic fertilizers do not meet the quantity required for large-scale commercial farming.

Shocks such as COVID-19 inevitably make markets volatile. The "Hamro Krishi" app supported by Nepal's Ministry of Agriculture and Livestock Development promotes climate-smart agriculture through agro-advisories to support farmers' decision-making. It provides a weekly weather bulletin and updated information on the market price of vegetables. The app was supposed to give farmers more negotiating power with local vendors, but women farmers' experiences show that information alone cannot ensure fair prices. A woman farmer in Kavre mentioned that the selling price of the vegetable was decided arbitrarily, based on profit margin by the vegetable vendor, intermediaries between farmers and markets, and hence, despite the app-provided market information, farmers do not have bargaining power over the intermediaries. This shows the limits of digital farming-advisory support. In addition, local-level regulatory mechanisms must be set up to ensure farmers get fair prices for their produce.

Research in times of COVID-19

Rapid and engaged research with the support of local NGOs on COVID-19 impacts on agrarian livelihoods shows various effects for women farmers. Women-led groups can help to overcome such crises as they interlink local food relief and equip women with "technical and managerial skills as well as political voice" (Agarwal, 2021). Women-centric initiatives and robust local networks require more research in order to understand locally experienced harms, but also hope, by understanding pathways of resilience.

As authors we acknowledge that we live, unlike many of our research subjects, with the "uncomfortable privilege" (Gonda et al., 2021) of being safe while we do not depend on daily wages or seasonal labor. In order to become more critically reflexive researchers, we would like to acknowledge our conflicting emotions and subjectivities as our work is inextricably linked to the uncertainty the village communities live with during COVID-19. This is part of an emancipatory process that embraces the interconnectedness of vulnerabilities and challenges in existing hegemonic knowledge-production practices (ibid.). Even among we four authors were discrepancies in communication as we are located in diverse institutional and regional settings during the pandemic: a national research organization, an international research-for-development organization, and a European university. However, the regular knowledge-sharing exchange via digital technologies made it possible for us to bring together voices from the field and government responses to develop our own critical perspectives and write this book chapter together. We hope that it does justice to the everyday challenges faced by women smallholders in Nepal, and that it reflects, globally, both harm and hope in challenging times.

References

Adhikari, Keshav, The Himalayan Times, April 19, 2020. Vegetables worth millions rotting in farms Amid lockdown in Dhading. Available at: https://cutt.ly /1xFLK47 Accessed on March 26, 2021.

Agarwal, B. (2021). Livelihoods in COVID times: Gendered perils and new pathways in India. *World Development, 139*. https://doi.org/10.1016/j.worlddev .2020.105312

Egger, D., Miguel, E., Warren, S. S., Shenoy, A., Collins, E., Karlan, D., Parkerson, D., Mobarak, A. M., Fink, G., Udry, C., Walker, M., Haushofer, J., Larreboure, M., Athey, S., Lopez-Pena, P., Benhachmi, S., Humphreys, M., Lowe, L., Meriggi, N. F., Wabwire, A., Davis, C. A., Pape, U. J., Graff, T., Voors, M., Nekesa, C., & Vernot, C. (2021). Falling living standards during the COVID-19 crisis: Quantitative evidence from nine developing countries. *Science Advances, 7*(6). https://doi.org/10.1126/sciadv.abe0997

Gonda, N., Leder, S., González-Hidalgo, M., Chiwona-Karltun, L., Stiernström, A., Hajdu, F., Fischer, K., Asztalos Morell, I., Kadfak, A., & Arvidsson, A. (2021). Critical Reflexivity in Political Ecology Research: How Can the Coronavirus Pandemic Transform Us into Better Researchers? *Frontiers in Human Dynamics*, *3*(41), 652968.

Government of Nepal (GoN) and World Bank (WB). (2020). Joint press release. [Online]. Available at: https://mof.gov.np/uploads/document/file/Joint%20PR _REED%20signing_20201222052149.pdf Accessed on 5.02.2021

Leder, S., Clement, F., & Karki, E. (2017). Reframing women's empowerment in water security programmes in Western Nepal. *Gender & Development*, *25*(2), 235–251. https://doi.org/10.1080/13552074.2017.1335452

Leder, S., Sugden, F., Raut, M., Ray, D., & Saikia, P. (2019). Ambivalences of collective farming: Feminist political ecologies from the Eastern Gangetic Plains. *International Journal of the Commons*, *13*(1), 105–129. https://doi.org /10.18352/ijc.917

Sharma, Namrata, Nepali Times, May 5, 2020. In Nepal lockdown, a domestic violence spike. Available at: https://www.nepalitimes.com/latest/in-nepal -lockdown-a-domestic-violence-spike/ Accessed on Feb. 25, 2021.

Poudel, Arjun, The Kathmandu Post, May 27, 2020. A 200 percent increase in maternal mortality since the lockdown began. Available at: https://tkpo.st /3eq7zuG Accessed on March 26, 2021.

Shrestha, G., & Clement, F. (2019). Unravelling gendered practices in the public water sector in Nepal. *Water Policy*, *21*(5), 1017–1033. https://doi.org/10.2166 /wp.2019.238

Sugden, F., Agarwal, B., Leder, S., Saikia, P., Raut, M., Kumar, A., & Ray, D. (2020). Experiments in farmer collectives in Eastern India and Nepal: Processes, benefits and challenges. *Journal of Agrarian Change*, *21*(4), 90–121. https://doi. org/10.1111/joac.12369

Shah, Arjun, The Kathmandu Post, Nov. 9, 2020. Sudurpaschim's agriculture subsidy plan for returnees falls short. Available at: rb.gy/qs7zvc Accessed on March 26, 2021.

Yadav, P. and Payal, P. 2020. The challenges that COVID-19 has brought to newly elected women leaders in Nepal. UCL IRDR Blog on June 22, 2020. Available at: https://cutt.ly/WxFLgm2 Accessed on March 26, 2021.

2 Gender implications of COVID-19 in Cambodia

Sovanneary Huot and Leif Jensen

The COVID-19 pandemic threatens the health and economy of all countries – large and small, rich and poor. Although the Cambodian government successfully averted widespread virus transmission in 2020, it has recently seen a spike in confirmed cases and deaths. COVID-19 poses the greatest challenge to the health and well-being of the Cambodian community, education system, and key engines of Cambodia's economy – garment, textiles, and footwear (GTF) manufacturing, tourism, construction, and agriculture. School closures profoundly impacted learning and assessment systems. About 39 percent of paid workers have been severely affected (World Bank 2020a). Lockdowns and social distancing restrictions broke the links between farmers and their markets, resulting in income loss. Rapid income decline creates panic and jeopardizes food security for vulnerable groups, including people with disabilities, children, migrant workers, older people, and woman-headed households. Here we focus on COVID-19's impacts on food security, consumption, and gender differences, especially among smallholder farmers. We first describe Cambodia's COVID-19 experience, then detail impacts of the pandemic on education, the garment industry, construction, tourism, and agriculture. Finally, we consider the government response to the pandemic.

COVID-19 in Cambodia

Cambodia's experience with COVID-19 has been dynamic. Immediately after a spike in March and April 2020, the government created the National Committee for COVID-19 Response, led by the Prime Minister, implementing school, business, and factory closures; international and domestic travel restrictions; mass gathering bans; social distancing; and mask mandates. The government collaborated with the Pasteur Institute in Cambodia, the World Health Organization (WHO), and the US Centers for Disease Control and Prevention to develop screening, tracing, testing, quarantine, and treatment to

DOI: 10.4324/9781003198277-3

limit virus transmission. The Khmer New Year holiday and the Water Festival were cancelled. As the infection rate declined during the third and fourth quarters of 2020, some restrictions were lifted, and limited economic activity in agriculture, manufacturing, and other sectors resumed. Public and private institutions and schools partially or fully reopened. Initial success reversed in spring 2021 with a spike in cases. The new B.1.1.7 variant spread quickly. As a result, although Cambodia reported relatively few cases in 2020, it is now catching up with its neighbors, with 2,378 cases and 11 deaths by March 30, 2021. Economic activity was curtailed anew, and all schools were ordered to fully close again on March 20, 2021. Although vaccinations began, only 401,972 vaccine doses had been administered by March 23, 2021.

Impacts on education

School closures profoundly impacted the education system, millions of students, and thousands of teachers and schools (MoEYS 2020). Standard learning systems and assessment forms were interrupted, with significant impacts on learning quality and human capital growth (World Bank 2020a). Digital education systems adopted to mitigate COVID-19 risk reach only the 20 percent of students with Internet access (CARE 2020). Unequal access to online learning materials disadvantages rural and economically vulnerable families. Mindful of such disparities, the Ministry of Education, Youth, and Sport (MoEYS 2020) delivered various forms of distance learning programs – via social media platforms, television, and radio – to keep kids learning during this unprecedented period.

There is a widening gender gap in access to education. Girls from rural and low-income families are at risk of having fewer opportunities to access school materials or return to school upon reopening. Some families experiencing economic hardship keep girls at home to help with household chores and childcare. Women bear a disproportionate burden from school closures with new care responsibilities for now out-of-school children and home schooling (UN 2020).

A school feeding program[1] in ten provinces also closed. During the first school closures, the World Feeding Program (WFP) partially continued with take-home meals to school children from the poorest households. When schools partially reopened, the program resumed but was threatened by the surge in cases.

Impacts of industry closures on income, remittances, and food security

GTF manufacturing, tourism, and construction were adversely affected (World Bank 2020b). Income and remittances declined, placing additional pressure on families, exacerbating declines in farm income and risks of food insecurity (Oxfam 2020). Factory and business closures compelled many migrant workers to return home, increasing household expenses. As of 2019, approximately 4.1 million rural individuals out-migrate for work annually, the majority to Phnom Penh's garment factories. Women outnumber men; young women comprise more than 80 percent of the GTF workforce. In addition to domestic labor migration, 2.5 million Cambodians live abroad, including 1.2 million Cambodian workers in Thailand. The pandemic left tens of thousands of migrant workers unemployed, eliminating overnight the remittances that keep many rural households afloat (ADB 2020). The unprecedented closures of workplaces in Thailand and the Thai-Cambodia border led to massive return migration. The government collaborated with the UN Joint Program[2] to protect migrant-sending communities from the virus by providing COVID-19 prevention information and health care services. Additionally, the program helped returned migrants cope with socioeconomic impacts. Vulnerable individuals, particularly women and woman-headed households, received economic reintegration packages, including grants for setting up small businesses, grocery stores, livestock raising, and other income-generating activities (IOM Cambodia 2020).

International travel restrictions and local lockdowns resulted in a collapse of tourism and hospitality services, causing around 11,000 tourism workers to lose their jobs (UN 2020). Closures of restaurants, tourist destinations, and businesses reduced food purchasing and demand for farm production. As reported by the UNDP Cambodia, Ms. Soda, deputy chief of Sovatepheap Thoamacheat Agricultural Cooperative, observed that

[b]efore COVID-19, we faced a supply shortage – we had access to markets but not enough vegetables. After COVID-19, it is the opposite: workers return [from the towns and cities] and begin to grow vegetables, but there are not enough buyers [due to reduced demand from restaurants, tourists etc.], so we then have a market surplus.

Members of this cooperative have had to settle for lower prices (UNDP Cambodia 2020).

Impacts on agriculture and smallholder farmers

The pandemic's effects on agriculture extend well beyond production for the devastated tourism industry. To ensure sufficient food for the population and avert high food prices, Cambodia's government, in April 2020, declared a ban on certain exports that has since been lifted. Social distancing restrictions and fear of the virus imposed additional constraints on smallholder farmers. Limited ability to sell their farm products led to decreased incomes (UN 2020). A study by Future Forum & Angkor Research (2020) indicates that smallholders in Siem Reap, Kampong Speu, and Kampot provinces saw painful income declines by 46, 46, and 29 percent, respectively. Income from selling vegetables, fruits, and aquaculture decreased by 32, 95, and 46 percent. Fortunately, income from selling paddy rice increased by 51 percent. Food purchasing patterns shifted toward staple foods over vegetables and fruits, reflecting heightened priority on household food security.

The COVID-19 pandemic has reinforced gender inequalities (Oxfam Cambodia 2020). Smallholder women farmers already have limited access to productive resources, services, technologies, markets, and investment capital and are more vulnerable to income loss (ADB 2020). Business and service closures increase the difficulty of selling their products, since women have limited access to markets and transportation compared to men. Weak demand for diverse crops forces women smallholders to sell their goods at lower prices. The income loss challenges continuation, not to mention expansion of their farming enterprises. To gain a comprehensive understanding of the hardships faced by women smallholder farmers, the lead author remotely interviewed farmers affiliated with the Women in Agriculture Network Project in Cambodia (WAgN-Cambodia).[3] A woman farmer of an agricultural cooperative (KKSRAC) in Siem Reap province reported that her family was severely affected by COVID-19. In the lockdown her husband and adult children lost their jobs. The closures led to an estimated 30–40 percent decrease in demand for her vegetables, a penalty worsened by lower prices for what she *could* sell (Figure 2.1).

Other women farmers in Battambang Province reported similar challenges and hardships. They sold their vegetables at a lower price and, consequently, lacked investment capital for the next growing season. A women farmer in Battambang lamented, "I felt really discouraged by the drop in prices we could get for whatever vegetables we have grown." They used to have several sources of income, including vegetable sales and remittances. Since the lockdown, their husbands and children returned home causing income losses and added expenses for food, medical care, and other household expenditures, simultaneously increasing care work for women (Figure 2.2).

Income decline decreases food security for vulnerable groups. A household survey found coping mechanisms among Cambodians experiencing income loss include reducing food and non-food consumption, buying food on credit, and borrowing from relatives and friends (Karamba et al. 2020). Elders are adversely affected, with 61 percent eating less food or consuming poorer quality food (HelpAge International 2020). Woman-headed households have experienced a higher rate of food insecurity during the

Figure 2.1 A Cambodian woman farmer. Smallholders have been especially hard hit by the pandemic (Phang Saret).

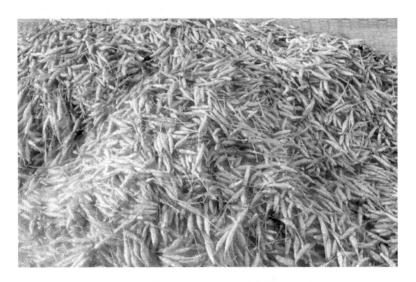

Figure 2.2 Chilis from a woman's farm in Battambang Province. Despite a reduced price, she finds it hard to sell them (Channaty Ngang).

pandemic than man-headed households. Over one-third of woman-headed households have faced moderate food insecurity compared to less than one-quarter among man-headed households (Future Forum & Angkor Research 2020). If prolonged, food insecurity and diets insufficient in micronutrients threaten the cognitive development of hundreds of thousands of children (UN 2020). The pandemic also heightened women's vulnerability to climate change. Notably, a massive flash flood occurred in October 2020 destroying thousands of homes and hectares of agricultural land. Negative impacts on shelter, agricultural production, food stocks and seed availability exacerbated already disadvantaged women's vulnerabilities (HRF 2021; ADB 2020). Reduced incomes mean less money for an adequate diet (HRF 2021).

Government response

The Cambodian government has taken some *economic recovery measures*, including reducing taxes, restructuring loans, and providing investment capital at low interest rates for small-, medium-, and large-sized farms, enterprises, or businesses. Intended to help farmers maintain production, small-scale farmers are less likely to benefit, often having less access to these loans compared to larger farms. For *livelihood coping assistance*, the government provided stimulus funds to 2.4 million poor and vulnerable households (UN 2020). Gender is not considered among eligibility criteria for this support; all registered poor and vulnerable households are entitled. However, the government offered additional support to pregnant women from impoverished households, hoping to reduce maternal and infant malnutrition. While some farmers would have qualified for the stimulus package funds, that program was more for emergency food relief based on their low income. It was not designed to help poor smallholders sustain their farms. The government has also taken *social protection measures* to support factory workers and tourism-related service workers temporarily laid off. A US$40 per month stimulus was provided to tourism-related service workers, while US$70 per month (US$40 from the government, US$30 by factory owners) was provided to factory workers (UN 2020). The coping assistance and social protection supports lasted from May to December 2020.

These programs only target poor households, formal sector workers, medium- and large-sized farms, or enterprises, excluding informal workers. Approximately 6.1 million informal workers (including smallholder farmers) have suffered from the pandemic but cannot benefit from the government's cash support (CARE 2020). An example is Srey Touch, a married woman with two small children, who lost her job as an entertainment worker when the virus hit, making her family homeless (Oxfam Cambodia

2021). A victim of domestic abuse and abandonment by her husband, she fought to survive by joining with other coworkers in filing for the government's National Social Security Fund. Unfortunately, their applications were denied given their status as informal workers. Things became more hopeful when Srey Touch joined the Cambodian Food and Service Workers Federation (CFSWF), which provides training in women's rights and gender equality. She empowered herself and worked to protect, support, and empower other women in the informal sector to acquire their rights. She now has proper shelter and enough nutritious food for her children. In her words:

> I have received a lot of new knowledge from various training by CFSWF. I've learnt about women's rights, gender-based violence, and social protection. It provides me a concrete foundation to speak up for my right as a woman and worker. I'm happy that I can use this knowledge to support other coworkers who are working in the entertainment sector like me.

In sum, the pandemic has profoundly disrupted all aspects of Cambodian life, including but not limited to economic opportunity, food security, time poverty, and social and psychological well-being. It has laid bare and exacerbated prevailing gender-based inequalities. Smallholder farmers have been severely affected by social distancing restrictions, while women smallholder farmers have faced greater challenges and more vulnerabilities to the socioeconomic crisis than their male counterparts.

Notes

1 WFP provided free meals to 280,000 school children in 1,113 pre-primary and primary schools across ten provinces in 2020.
2 The UN Joint Program in Cambodia was created by four agencies – WHO, UNFPA, UNICEF, and IOM – and funded by the COVID-19 Multi Partner Trust Fund (MPTF).
3 The WAgN-Cambodia project was designed by Penn State University researchers and partners to empower women and improve the nutrition status of women and children in Cambodia with support from the USAID-funded Sustainable Intensification Innovation Lab (SIIL) at Kansas State University. Both authors were part of this project.

References

ADB 2020. *Proposed countercyclical support facility loan Kingdom of Cambodia: COVID-19 active response and expenditure support program* [online]. Available from: COVID-19 Active Response and Expenditure Support Program: Report and Recommendation of the President (adb.org) [accessed 25 July, 2020].

CARE 2020. *Rapid gender analysis during COVID-19 pandemic, mekong subregional report Cambodia, Lao People's Democratic Republic, Myanmar, Thailand and Viet Nam* [online]. Available from: Regional-Mekong-Rapid-Gender-Analysis_COVID-19_Final_September2020.pdf (reliefweb.int) [accessed 17 October 2020].

FAO 2020a. *COVID-19 and smallholder producers' access to markets*. Rome: FAO. doi:10.4060/ca8657en.

Future Forum & Angkor Research 2020. *Covid-19 gender analysis at the household and wage worker level* [online]. Available from: Publications (angkorresearch.com) [accessed 25 July, 2020].

HelpAge International 2020. *COVID-19 rapid needs assessment of older people July 2020* [online]. Available from: covid19-rapid-needs-assessment--asia-pacific--region.pdf (helpage.org) [accessed 15 March, 2021].

HRF 2021. *Floods response plan: Cambodia* [online]. Available from: PowerPoint Presentation (reliefweb.int) [accessed 27 February, 2021].

IOM Cambodia 2020. *COVID-19 response: Situation report* [online]. Available from: C:\Users\MWALKO~1\AppData\Local\Temp\mso936A.tmp (iom.int) [accessed 28 January, 2021].

Karamba, W., Nkengene, C.T., and Tong, K. 2020. *The socioeconomic impacts of COVID-19 on households in Cambodia. The high-frequency phone survey of households round 1*. World Bank Group [online]. Available from World Bank Document [accessed 25 March, 2021].

MoEYS 2020. *Cambodia education response plan to COVID 19 pandemic*. Phnom Penh, Cambodia [online]. Available from: Cambodia Education Response Plan to COVID-19 Pandemic July 2020 (moeys.gov.kh) [accessed 25 July, 2020].

Oxfam Cambodia 2020. *The impact of COVID-19 on Cambodia's most vulnerable populations* [online]. Available from: Oxfam_Brief – The impact of Covid-19_LV06 (oi-files-cng-prod.s3.amazonaws.com) [accessed 15 March, 2021].

Oxfam Cambodia 2021. *A Women's struggle with COVID-19: on story of survival, strength and hope* [online]. Available from: A Woman's Struggle with Covid-19: a Story of Survival, Strength and Hope | Oxfam in Cambodia [accessed 15 March, 2021].

UNDP Cambodia 2020. *Living in rural Cambodia during COVID-19: Examples from farming communities* [online]. Available from: Living in Rural Cambodia during COVID-19: Examples from Farming Communities | UNDP in Cambodia [accessed 27 February, 2021].

UN 2020. *UN Cambodia framework for the immediate socio-economic response to COVID-19* [online]. Available from: KHM_Socioeconomic_Response-Plan_2020.pdf (un.org) [accessed 27 February, 2021].

Oxfam Cambodia 2020. *The impact of COVID-19 on Cambodia's most vulnerable populations* [online]. Available from: Oxfam_Brief – The impact of Covid-19_LV06 (oi-files-cng-prod.s3.amazonaws.com) [accessed 15 March, 2021].

Oxfam Cambodia 2021. *A Women's struggle with COVID-19: on story of survival, strength and hope* [online]. Available from: A Woman's Struggle with Covid-19:

a Story of Survival, Strength and Hope | Oxfam in Cambodia [accessed 15 March, 2021].

WHO 2021. WHO Coronavirus (COVID-19) dashboard [online]. Available from: Cambodia: WHO Coronavirus Disease (COVID-19) Dashboard | WHO Coronavirus Disease (COVID-19) Dashboard [accessed 25 March, 2021].

World Bank 2020a. *Cambodian economic update: Cambodia in the time of COVID-19.* Washington, DC: World Bank Group.

World Bank 2020b. *Cambodian economic update: Restrained Recovery.* Washington, DC: World Bank Group.

WFP Cambodia 2021. *Cambodia country brief February 2021.* [online]. Available from: https://docs.wfp.org/api/documents/WFP-0000125049/download/?_ga =2.92684445.1426877709.1616617611-1170571446.1611447354 [accessed 15 March 2021].

3 COVID-19, India, small-scale farmers, and indigenous Adivasi communities – the answer to the future lies in going back to the basics

Regina Hansda

Introduction

India has experienced one of the worst devastations to life and livelihoods from COVID-19. Part of the disaster and devastation has been human-made. Lack of planning and preparation by the central government for tackling the COVID-19 pandemic dealt a massive blow to India's economy and caused enormous hardships to the poor and the vulnerable. The informal rural economy and the agriculture sector have been hardest hit (Singh, 2020). Central government's refusal to acknowledge the scale of the crisis and their mismanagement handling the medical emergency-turned-human-itarian crisis aggravates people's suffering and has deepened the crisis further. Both the first national lockdown announced in the last week of March 2020 with four hours of notice and the second wave of the pandemic have left devastation and grief of unimagined proportions. Two very grim and distressing images on national television and social media captured the imagination of the country and form a part of the collective failure and helplessness: first, the image of returning migrants with their young and old from the cities to the villages, walking thousands of miles for days with their minimal belongings; and, second, the image of the gasping COVID-19 patients, lack of hospital beds and oxygen, and family members and relatives grieving the loss of their loved ones. Minimal reporting from the rural areas suggests that the situation is likely worse, considering the health infrastructure in the rural areas in ordinary times is inadequate. Both situations, spread over a year, show how the state abdicated its responsibilities for food security and public health, leaving individuals to fend for themselves.

This chapter focuses on the implications of food and livelihood insecurity on the poor and vulnerable sections of society. I demonstrate how

DOI: 10.4324/9781003198277-4

government and its various institutions not only abdicated their responsibilities toward their citizens; instead, the pandemic was used as an opportunity to further dispossess and erode farmers', especially poor, Dalit, and Adivasi (indigenous peoples's), rights and resources. I argue that food and health is linked, and future farming and livelihoods for small-scale farmers and indigenous communities lies in going back to basics. By basics, I mean resisting, maintaining, and claiming what belongs to the community (knowledge systems, resources, and practices) so that power remains in the hands of the people and communities.

COVID-19 lockdown, migrant crisis, food and livelihood insecurity issues

The first COVID-19 lockdown triggered a large-scale trend of reverse migration across the country. As per the World Bank study (Ratha et al., 2020), roughly 40 million internal migrants (inter and intrastate) were affected by the lockdown. The countryside, for a change, became the site of hope for many. The main reasons for return migration on such a scale were the loss of livelihoods in the cities, inadequate savings to tide people over this crisis period, and staring at an uncertain future. Most of these homeward-bound migrants walking hundreds of miles on foot had one common refrain: "we don't know whether we will die of coronavirus, but we will certainly die of hunger." The food insecurity issues were massive and to some extent addressed by various citizens' groups and extra government rations (e.g., 5 kg of rice per household); but the experiences have been varied and inadequate in most areas.

The worst part of the countrywide lockdown, which kept extending in phases, was that it coincided with the country's peak harvesting season for a variety of crops (winter crops, wheat and barley – March–April; summer crops, vegetables and fruits – March–June). With the country coming to a sudden halt and disruption to supply chains, not only did all the hard work of farmers go to waste, but the pattern of labor-flow for the peak paddy season in the monsoons (rice/paddy; June–July) was disrupted (Figures 3.1 and 3.2). Agriculturally prosperous states like Punjab, Haryana, and Maharashtra witnessed labor shortages, while states like Bihar, Jharkhand, and Madhya Pradesh experienced a surge in the labor pool, which posed additional challenges to employment opportunities locally. The pandemic disrupted remittances, which migrants regularly sent to their households, affecting access to the everyday needs around food, nutrition, and health care of those who were in their home villages.

Figure 3.1 Paddy harvesting, Bihar (Regina Hansda).

Figure 3.2 Paddy threshing, Bihar (Regina Hansda).

Impact of COVID-19 on rural women and inadequacy of government measures

A study conducted by the *Mahila Kisan Adhikaar Manch* (MAKAAM) – Forum for Women Farmers' Rights – across caste groups in the 17 districts of Maharashtra on the impact of COVID-19 and the lockdown on single women farmers and wage laborers found that overall food consumption declined in this period. "About 45 percent of women did not get a single day of work in the 50 days of the lockdown." Those with ration cards, apart from receiving their quota of rice and wheat at subsidised price, received additional food grains, but for a limited period of time (MAKAAM, 2020). SEWA-Bharat (2020) interviewed 300 women members in April–May in 12 states across 20 trades and found that only 5 percent were earning anything after lockdown. The government of India announced several relief measures for the returning migrants and farmers. However, because of inadequate gender considerations in planning and/or corruption issues, women farm workers stood the least chance to benefit from these measures. For instance, under the Pradhan Mantri Kisan Samman Nidhi (PM-KISAN) scheme with an allocated budget of Rs 1.7 lac crore (US$25 billion), a small portion of that amount, Rs. 6,000 (US$80.5), is meant to be provided to the small and marginal farmers as financial assistance during the lockdown (Varshney et al., 2021). However, the eligibility criteria for this scheme is land ownership and deed (*patta*) papers in the name of the applicant. In a country where 76 percent of women engaged in agriculture sector own about 13 percent of the agricultural land, this scheme excludes more than 87 percent of small and marginal women farmers, many of whom are landless.[1] A small enquiry from a field site in Bihar, where I attempted to match the online government data[2] with on-the-ground experiences of women farmers revealed gross corruption and mismanagement. For instance, the name of a beneficiary who I personally know from my ethnographic fieldwork was reflected thrice in the government website. Once, ascribing her gender as "male,' second as "female," and, on the third occasion, the gender was missing. There were many such repeated, misspelt names, and missing genders. This beneficiary list is a sad retelling of the jugglery that goes on in data manipulation and statistics to misappropriate government funds. Not only are such funds not utilized fully and properly, but the needs of the women farmers and agricultural laborers remain unattended.

In addition, the domestic became the site of healing, recovery, and care with an additional work burden on women in the rural areas. The domestic also became the site of increased domestic violence, which many saw as an additional health risk for women (Ghoshal, 2020). A few field contacts in telephone interviews indicated how agricultural laborers, who are mostly women, worked at almost half the wage rate during the paddy transplantation and harvesting season. For instance, the usual pattern of wage payment for agricultural labor work in Gaya district, my research site, is by both cash and kind, with kind payment often acting as the preferred mode of payment. The going rate for kind payment is 5 kg of rice (during transplantation), and one bundle on every 11 bundles of harvested paddy (*gyarah gaahi mein ek gaahi*) for the landholding farmer. The pandemic saw a breakdown of the village moral economy. The monsoons were good, they came on time, and despite the relative surplus production from the previous year, the agricultural workers were paid less. The few generous landholding farmers who occasionally would pay extra wages or share produce from their kitchen gardens (e.g., banana, or chicken to be shared by the laborers after harvest) preferred not to, as a cautionary measure. This cautious approach meant additional food security implications for the wage workers who are mostly from Dalit communities. In addition, the employment under Mahatma Gandhi National Rural Employment Guarantee Act (MNREGA), which guarantees 100 days of rural employment to interested wage workers from each household, witnessed an increasing surge in demand because of the returnee migrants and the State's inability to keep pace with the demand. With the increase in unpaid work, and the absence of support from male family members, women's mental and physical exhaustion have been aggravated by the lack of food, income, and an uncertain future. Single women households, with a limited social network and no savings, have been the worst affected (Dutta, Agarwal and Sivakami, 2020).

Impact on indigenous Adivasi women

A significant population of Adivasis are dependent on forest-based livelihoods and were impacted heavily by the lockdown. The non-wood forest products (NWFPs) that are utilized and commercialized are seasonal in nature, with more than half of their annual income accruing during the months of March to June, which is also the lean period for them. This year it coincided with the lockdown period. Some of the harvested NWFPs (mostly leaves, tubers, green leafy vegetables, fruits, and berries) include tendu leaves (*Diospyros melanoxylon*), wild honey, tamarind, mango, sal leaves, sal seeds, mahua flowers, mahua seeds, and achaar seeds amongst others. Many of these NWFPs are food items consumed for household food and nutrition security needs, with the surplus sold in the local markets or to the government procurement agencies. The cash earned during these months is critical for sustenance during the monsoon season when employment dries up. However, because of the lockdown restrictions, both the government procurement agencies as well as the local traders delayed their procurement, or procured far less than usual, or at a distress-sale rate, thereby risking the livelihoods of millions of forest-dependent communities.

The pandemic as an opportunity to erode farmers and Adivasi people's rights

The government's lockdown mantra has been *"Aapda mein avsar"* (opportunity in crisis) and such a philosophy and outlook has resulted in initiatives and outcomes that have adversely affected the farming sector and the Adivasi people. For instance, the pandemic saw the institution of the three New Farm Laws without much debate and discussion in parliament. Also, large-scale clearances to environmental projects have adversely impacted the Adivasi people.

The three Farm Laws[3] and farmers' resistance

The government claims that the three newly constituted Farm Laws are designed to modernize the farming sector and to double farmers' incomes. The farmer protests where women farmers have played a pro-active and leading role suggest otherwise. After more than six months of protests, the battle between the government and the farmers on the Farm Laws is on, on the outskirts of Delhi, and it appears likely to continue until a reasonable resolution. The farmers who resist are from states which have been the sites of the Green Revolution (Punjab, Haryana, and Western Uttar Pradesh). These farmers have experienced the "modern methods" of farming and its associated increased farm productivity and profitability. But along with increased prosperity, they have also witnessed the destruction of the ecological basis for farming (e.g., declining soil fertility, depleting water table) (Sidhu and Dhillon, 1997). The farmers in these areas are aware of the inappropriateness of the mono-cropping systems that they have been practicing, the artificiality of subsidies on agro-chemicals, and how it is only the guaranteed minimum support price and the Mandi system that has kept such a system of farming alive. So why are these farmers protesting in a do-or-die kind of battle? Why is there an outpouring of national and international solidarity to their cause?[4] It is the belief that these Farm Laws are formulated to streamline greater capital accumulation by corporations without safeguards for the farmers; it is the fear of indebtedness and the fear of losing the freedom to practice farming on their own terms (Bhattacharya and Patel, 2021). Moreover, the New Farm Laws, by the very nature of their ambiguity and lack of social protection, foreclose the possibilities of farmers returning to sustainable methods of farming. What lessons can be drawn from these farmers' protest for the farming sector in general, and especially for resource-starved small-scale farmers? In simple words, they must hold on to their land and farming systems until and unless a clear blueprint and pathway for their transition and progression to alternative sources of livelihoods are planned by policymakers.

Indigenous communities, COVID-19, and continued state repression

Under cover of the pandemic both overt and covert land grabs have been ongoing in the tribal hinterlands in the name of development works such as plantations (Sushmita, 2020, 2021), mining (Agarwal, 2020), and hydroelectric projects (Pinto and Van Adhikar Media Team, 2020). Attempts to resist the slow encroachment of Adivasi land has met with brutal police assaults and death. For instance, in a recent face-off in Bastar forests against road construction where three people died, one of the witnesses, Krishna Kadti, 18, a Class 12 student from Jagargunda shares:

> we were beaten up by the security forces when we went to submit our demands. They beat us earlier too. We also got angry and some of our people pelted stones at their vehicles and at the camp. First, the security personnel threw tear gas bombs, and then opened fire.
>
> (Verma, 2021)

Similarly, on the issue of livelihoods, Rajanti Malik from Kandhamahal district, Odisha, shares the ordeal of her community:

> In the midst of this lockdown, while we were told to stay at home, the forest department destroyed and cleared our natural forests. They came and cleared the existing forest, on which we depend for food and livelihood, to plant other trees (afforestation under CAMPA) ... Due to the coronavirus lockdown, we couldn't even sell our Siali leaf and Sal leaf plates, Tendu or Bahada and all of these are getting spoiled. We are feeling helpless and are unable to understand how to feed and safeguard our children. In this crisis, between lockdown restrictions and the Forest Department actions, we are helpless. How will we survive?
>
> (Pinto and Dubey, 2020)

For most of these projects, the government gave speedy environmental clearances without any field visits or due process such as stakeholder consultations, environmental and social impact assessments and based their decisions only on reports submitted by the project proponents. In addition, they arrested leading Adivasi environmental activists (e.g., Hidme Markam), who have been keeping a constant community vigil on state and corporate aggression of their land and forests, on concocted charges during the pandemic.

Going back to the basics to strengthen rural communities and women farmers

COVID-19 should be seen as a wake-up call for humanity, to reflect on and rethink the rural. The pandemic in general reminds us any disruptions and shocks disproportionately affect the already disadvantaged. It has also shaken the uncontested idea that the future lies in the urban, and in the cities and that work and leisure cannot be organized in a more carbon-efficient way. The pandemic provides us with the opportunity to rethink, reclaim, and redesign food systems that can ensure safe, healthy, sustainable, and resilient communities that recognize and build on local knowledge systems and practices. However, without addressing the central questions around land and tenurial security of the peasantry, any progress is likely to be peripheral and temporary.

Addressing landlessness, food insecurity through land reforms, and access to forest rights

Landlessness is a massive issue in India. According to the 2011 Socio-Economic and Caste Census, 56 percent of households in rural India do not own any agricultural land. Landless farmers are disproportionately women, and belong to the Dalit and Adivasi communities. These two categories and mostly women from Dalit and Adivasi communities comprise the bulk of the laboring class in agriculture and allied activities. Many of the relief and recovery measures promoted by the government automatically exclude most women smallholders, tenant farmers, sharecroppers, and daily agricultural wage laborers. The only way to redress this inequity and reduce the marginalization of the poor and the vulnerable is through seeking creative ways of land redistribution. In the case of Adivasis, it is important that the inalienable forest rights of the Adivasi communities are upheld and maintained by all concerned. The Adivasis must resist all attempts at state appropriation of their lands and territories. In addition, the wider public must question respective governments and make them accountable for all the state-mediated violence in the Adivasi and tribal areas, including all attempts by governments to dilute environmental laws which create an easy pathway for corporate land grabs.

Encouraging agro-ecological farming for long-term sustainability and resilience

Food insecurity has been one of the main concerns of this pandemic and it has been articulated by multiple food activists and agencies like FAO, IFAD, and La Via Campesina, among others. With the closing of borders and disruption of supply chains, one of the main lessons of the pandemic is the importance of locally produced food, especially vegetables and fruit. There is increasing recognition that by boosting investment for agroecology in the rural areas we can feed the world and strengthen our resilience against this crisis, and those yet to come. As food supply chains break down, community supported agriculture (CSA) shows us the way. For instance, the North East Slow Food & Agrobiodiversity Society (NESFAS), Meghalaya, through their weekly market in the last couple of years serves as an effective platform for producers and consumers to come together and buy and sell organically produced indigenous food crops, including, different varieties of wild edibles. The COVID-19 lockdown disrupted this platform. However, some women farmers, who are also part of the participatory guarantee scheme were able to improvise and create an alternative supply chain through the "Farm on wheels" initiative, enabling access to their produce by willing consumers. There are many such small, local, individual, as well as community, initiatives that require incentivization and support. Studies point to more women-centric group approaches as new pathways for a post-COVID-19 future (Agarwal, 2021).

Going beyond rhetoric to reality

One of the clarion calls given during the pandemic by the Indian prime minister was the idea of *Atmanirbharta* – which means striving toward self-sufficiency. Contrary to what the three New Farm Laws claim, one of the ways of addressing the impending challenge of food insecurity and the protracted conditions of agrarian crisis in the country is to recognize the value of diverse, small-scale, sustainable food production systems across diverse agro-climatic zones instead of paving the way for corporate agriculture. The skill sets and knowledge of farming rests with the rural farming community, many of whom are marginal and small farmers, and it is incumbent upon governments to recognize the need for supporting food production systems that cater to their needs and interests. In addition, it is critical that the central questions around land access and tenurial security of farmers, across various intersections (gender, caste, class, ethnicity, religion, marital status) are addressed. Robust investments are needed for research and development that support and encourage small-scale farming. Policies are needed that protect and enhance marginal Adivasi and Dalit women's access to forests and other communal resources (water, grazing land) without dispossessing and eroding their rights.

Conclusion

In the past year since the COVID-19 lockdown it has become abundantly clear that the state abdicated its responsibility toward its citizens as far as food/livelihood security and public health is concerned. The resistance to the three New Farm Laws, with proactive participation and leadership by women farmers across caste and class, is an indication of the breakdown of trust between farmers and the government. Similarly, the Adivasis, with proactive leadership from women across the central Indian states over decades, have been resisting the imposition of the dominant development paradigm that undermines their foodways and ways of life, which are based on sustainable harvesting practices. It is pertinent to remind ourselves that a fair and just future is only possible when those most vulnerable have meaningful participation and a say in the transition process of the new imagined nation.

Notes

1 Landesa report: Land matters: Success stories of women land owners in India.
2 https://pmkisan.gov.in/Rpt_BeneficiaryStatus_pub.aspx
3 The New Farm Laws deal with production, storage, and marketing of farm produce.
4 Tweets by Rihanna and Greta Thunberg and other activists, academics, and policymakers.

References

Agarwal, B., 2021. Livelihoods in COVID times: Gendered perils and new pathways in India. *World Development*, 139, p.105312.

Agarwal, M. 2020. India's mining sector: Present is tense and future could be imperfect. https://india.mongabay.com/2020/07/indias-mining-sector-present-is-tense-and-future-could-be-imperfect/ Accessed on 4 May, 2021.

Bhattacharya, S. and Patel, U., 2021. Farmers' agitation in India due to audacious Farm Bill of 2020. *International Journal of Research in Engineering, Science and Management*, 4(1), pp. 35–37.

Chopra, D., 2014. 'They Don't Want to Work' versus 'They Don't Want to Provide Work': Seeking explanations for the decline of MGNREGA in Rajasthan.

Dutta, M., Agarwal, D. and Sivakami, M., 2020. The "invisible" among the marginalised: Do gender and intersectionality matter in the Covid-19 response?. *Indian Journal of Medical Ethics*, 5(4), pp. 302–308.

Ghoshal, R., 2020. Twin public health emergencies: Covid-19 and domestic violence. *Indian Journal of Medical Ethics*, 5, pp. 1–5.

Kumar, S. and Choudhury, S., 2021. Migrant workers and human rights: A critical study on India's COVID-19 lockdown policy. *Social Sciences & Humanities Open*, 3(1), p. 100130.

Landesa report (undated). Land matters: Success stories of women land owners in India.

MAKAAM, 2020. Unlocking the Crisis: Understanding impacts of COVID −19 and subsequent lockdown on single women farmers of Maharashtra. June 2020.

Pinto, A. and Dubey, S., June 2020. Adivasi and forest dwelling women across India face the brunt of the Covid Pandemic: Voices from the Ground Part-1. https://www.behanbox.com/adivasi-and-forest-dwelling-women-across-india-face-the -brunt-of-the-covid-pandemic-voices-from-the-ground/ Accessed on 31 March, 2021.

Pinto and Van Adhikar Media Team, 2020. "How the Government Diluted Forest Rights of Adivasis During Lockdown." Behar Box, July 19, 2020.

Ratha, D. K., De, S., Kim, E. J., Plaza, S., Seshan, G. K. and Yameogo, N. D., 2020. *COVID 19 crisis through a migration lens* (No. 147828, pp. 1–50). The World Bank, April.

SEWA-Bharat, 2020. Gendered precarity in the lockdown. http://www.sewabha ratresearch.org/wp-content/uploads/2020/05/Gendered_Precarity_SB_Lock down-1.pdf

Sidhu, R. S. and Dhillon, M. S., 1997. Land and water resources in Punjab: Their degradation and technologies for sustainable use. *Indian Journal of Agricultural Economics*, 52(3), pp. 508–518.

Sushmita, 2020. Pandemic unleashes fresh hell for India's adivasis. *The Third Pole*. https://www.thethirdpole.net/en/livelihoods/pandemic-unleashes-fresh-hell-for -indias-adivasis/ Accessed on 4 April, 2021.

Sushmita, 2021. Plantations over people: India's Covid-19 recovery plan for indigenous groups. https://www.thethirdpole.net/en/livelihoods/plantations-over -people-indias-covid-19-recovery-plan-for-indigenous-groups/ Accessed on 18 May, 2021.

Singh, B. P., 2020. Impact of COVID-19 on rural economy in India. MPRA Paper 100530, University Library of Munich, Germany.

Varshney, D., Kumar, A., Mishra, A. K., Rashid, S. and Joshi, P. K., 2021. India's COVID-19 social assistance package and its impact on the agriculture sector. *Agricultural Systems*, 189, p. 103049.

Verma, G. 2021. Chhattisgarh: Three dead in firing on protest, villagers dig heels in at Sukma security camp. *MSN News*. https://www.msn.com/en-in/news/other /chhattisgarh-three-dead-in-firing-on-protest-villagers-dig-heels-in-at-sukma -security-camp/ar-BB1gSMaU Accessed on 20 May, 2021.

Zaidi, M., Chigateri, S., Chopra, D. and Roelen, K., 2017. "My Work Never Ends": Women's experiences of balancing unpaid care work and paid work through WEE programming in India. IDS Working Paper 494, Brighton: IDS.

4 Social aspects of women's agribusiness in times of COVID-19 in the Central Highlands of Vietnam

Nozomi Kawarazuka and Pham Thi Hoa

Introduction

Vietnam is considered one of the most successful countries in controlling the COVID-19 pandemic. By March 24, 2021, there were 2,576 cases and 35 deaths (Worldometers, 2021). We feel safe in Vietnam. Watching news on the global pandemic is like watching a scary movie from a different planet. Nevertheless, many Vietnamese people have been directly and indirectly affected by the pandemic. According to the General Statistics Office, 32.1 million Vietnamese workers either lost their jobs or had their working hours/salaries reduced in 2020 (Nguyen, 2021). Furthermore, over 75,000 Vietnamese were repatriated from 59 countries with 260 repatriation flights in 2020. Returned migrants included 219 male construction workers from Equatorial Guinea, of whom 129 were COVID positive, over 200 pregnant women from Taiwan, 53 infants from South Korea, and nearly 200 monks and nuns from India (Anh, 2020). These statistics demonstrate how intertwined the lives of Vietnamese workers are with the global economy.

At the global level, this pandemic has reconfirmed that current expression of neoliberal capitalism is inherently unequal and persistently excludes marginalized social groups during crisis (e.g., Stevano et al., 2021). We observe its wide range of economic and social consequences on marginalized people all over the world, especially women and children from disadvantaged backgrounds. The pandemic uncovered contradictions and conflicts within neoliberal capitalism for global growth and international development. Clearly productivity- and profit-focused economies are incompatible with equality, social welfare, and environmental sustainability. An urgent need exists for alternatives, including agrifood systems, that produce equitable distribution and sustainable utilization of labor and natural resources.

This chapter illustrates three women agribusiness owners in the Central Highlands whose business goals are not solely about profit and productivity, but more about social development and environmental sustainability.

DOI: 10.4324/9781003198277-5

The study draws on feminist approaches to entrepreneurship in terms of concepts and methodologies (Ahl, 2006; Hughes et al., 2012). We observe the social aspects of their businesses that determined the impacts of and responses to the COVID-19 pandemic. Their narratives suggest ideas to critically think what future alternative resilient agribusiness should aim for, and how social research can contribute to enriching understanding of women entrepreneurs.

Local context and methods

Lam Dong province is located in the Central Highlands of Vietnam and is well known for high-quality agricultural produce: vegetables, roots, tubers, flowers, fruits, coffee, tea, and dairy. Many Vietnamese consumers associate the name of the provincial capital, Da Lat city, with positive images of clean, high-quality, and fresh produce. The outskirts of Da Lat city offer an all-embracing view of greenhouses covering hundreds of hectares of irrigated farmlands (Figures 4.1 and 4.2). The province also has forest

Figure 4.1 The view of greenhouses from the outskirts of Da Lat city (Pham Thi Hoa).

Figure 4.2 Women work in a greenhouse for chrysanthemum cultivation, Lam Dong province, Vietnam (Pham Thi Hoa).

conservation areas where ethnic minority rangers monitor illegal wildlife poaching and maintain forests by planting trees.

The economic impact of COVID-19 on the Lam Dong horticultural industry was particularly serious for the cut-flower market, while impacts on other horticultural produce, especially the domestic market, remained relatively small and short. At the beginning of the pandemic, when the government closed borders, those selling vegetables and flowers for export lost their market. In the summer of 2020, when Vietnam had an outbreak in the central city of Da Nang, the horticultural sector was more significantly affected by the closure of domestic transport routes and reduced consumer demand especially from events, festivals, hotels, and domestic tourism. Agribusiness owners in Lam Dong adapted rapidly by looking for new markets online and finding retailers and individual consumers through Facebook, laying off some workers and shifting crops from export to domestic markets to adapt to domestic needs. The ability to adapt to change varies. Some agribusiness companies and their contract farmers/workers and traders were affected more seriously than others.

Three women respondents were selected from the list of 11 women agribusiness owners whom the second author met earlier during her study on the impact of COVID-19 on agriculture. The three women have different business histories and family backgrounds. Each agribusiness owner is unique, and their stories are not generalizable, yet their narratives illuminate agribusiness from women's perspectives. Prior to the interviews, respondents shared information about their agribusiness. In-depth interviews were conducted in late February 2021 in their homes or gardens. The first author participated in the interview online while the second author had face-to-face interactions. Each interview took one to one and a half hours using seven guiding questions. Topics included family, life history, business history, their informal support, relationships with employees, ethics, values and goals of their business, and their principles in decision-making related to their agribusiness. The interviewer took care to create a natural conversation format. Interviews were not recorded but documented as field notes. A thematic content analysis identified key non-economic aspects of agribusiness commonly observed among three respondents.

Stories

Respondents' responses to COVID-19

Lan,[1] 54, started her small agribusiness with coffee trees and tomatoes in 1990 when she married and had a first daughter. In 1992, she resigned from her professional job as a gynecologist to focus on her agribusiness. Over 30 years, she expanded her business to 27 hectares, hiring 100 workers, some of whom have worked for her for over 20 years. Her husband, a telecommunication engineer, resigned from his job and joined her business in 1999. Currently, they grow flowers and vegetables for domestic and global markets such as Japan, Singapore, and the Netherlands.

For Lan, this crisis is not the first time she faced a challenge. In 1999, with a sharp decline in global coffee prices, she cut down her trees and turned to flower production. This time with COVID-19, fresh-flower sales were seriously affected by reduced demand from hotels, events, and festival organizers in both domestic and global markets. She turned 30 percent of her flower farms over to vegetables, with the same brave and immediate decision as she had taken many years previously. This strategy worked well. Over the 2020 COVID-19 period, her greenhouse vegetable area expanded from 5 to 7 ha as she saw strong consumer demand for certified clean and safe vegetables. Lan also asked her daughter to establish online Facebook trading for the flowers to explore new business partners, particularly retailers rather than wholesalers. This enabled her to diversify her markets and find new regular customers, as a positive legacy of COVID-19.

Bich, 71, started farming in 2010 by renting a small farmland, in the year she lost everything: her real estate business went bankrupt; she sold her land; and she divorced her husband. She started farming for survival with no money, no land, no family support, and no knowledge of agribusiness. After three years, she began a hydroponic clean vegetable producing system through technical support from a Dutch private plant-breeding company (Rijk Zwaan). Currently she owns 1.8 ha of hydroponics cultivation areas and produces 180 tons of vegetables annually. She eventually gained a strong positive reputation and the trust of major local and foreign-invested supermarkets with a successful branding of her vegetables as safe and clean produce. She hires 20 workers, 70 percent of whom are ethnic minorities.

Bich planned to export her fresh vegetable to Japan during the 2020 Tokyo Olympics and in 2018 two Japanese middlemen visited her farms. She was excited and prepared for export. However, because of the pandemic, the Olympic games were postponed. Domestic demand in Da Nang also declined for two months during the second COVID-19 wave. She had nowhere to sell and had to reduce production. While her profit has reduced significantly, she kept her 20 workers' salaries at the same level and only reduced their bonus at the end of the year.

Hang, 42, a civil servant, produces environmentally sustainable coffee by hiring local farmers and sells high-quality roasted coffee directly to domestic consumers and baristas in Hanoi and Ho Chi Minh city. She started growing coffee in 2013 after she divorced her husband. With a minimum investment from her savings, she rented 2 ha of farm and planted local variety coffee trees, which she grows without chemicals. She eventually expanded her farms to 5 ha and tried many methods to roast coffee beans. Currently she hires five farmers and produces 2 tons of coffee beans per year. Her main job remains being a civil servant in Da Lat.

Like the horticulture and flower industries, around the world the coffee industry has been affected by COVID-19. Many Vietnamese coffee farmers have been unable to sell all their beans and have reduced incomes. Hang's coffee business is different. Her business and her farmers were not affected. Instead, demand from individual consumers increased during the stay-home period because her business and her coffee farmers are independent from the global coffee market.

Why did Lan and Bich not reduce their workers' salaries or lay some off as many companies have done? Why was Hang's business so strong compared to the global coffee industry in general? In the following sections we explore social aspects of their business management to understand the strategies that might have helped them to navigate challenges during COVID-19.

Informal support for building trust and making economic gains

These three women commonly utilize informal social networks to receive technical and psychological support, which is a foundation for building social trust and making economic gains for resiliency to crises such as the pandemic. Prior to their agribusiness, they had no knowledge or skills of agriculture or entrepreneurism. Lan was a gynecologist who became an English teacher. Bich's professional career was in real estate. Hang is a civil servant. However, they each utilized their social networks of friends, neighbors, and foreigners who provide psychological and technical support. We observed that they are open to new technologies and practices and have strong determination to continually innovate.

At the beginning of her business, Lan visited the largest flower garden in Da Lat with her husband to learn how to grow flowers. She soon realized the importance of quality seeds. She researched and identified companies in the Netherlands and imported her first batch of 1,500 seedlings in 1999. She then contacted a food consultancy company in Vietnam (Fresh Studio) and bought high-quality clean seed potatoes from them. She also received funds for training in the Netherlands and learnt Dutch technology, investing in a laboratory to propagate flowers by the in-vitro method. She established a demonstration area to share her technology with visitors, students, and young business owners. Although she had little knowledge and skills in horticultural business, informal social networks enabled her enterprise to grow and be resilient to shocks.

Bich's skills and knowledge of farming derived from childhood experience helping on the family farm. She aimed to produce clean and safe vegetables. She joined a training program in Malaysia organized by Rijk Zwaan, where she encountered hydroponic vegetable cultivation techniques. The hydroponic system does not use pesticides and has no waste, which ideally suited her aims. Upon returning from the training, she was determined to establish this system in her farm. It was her determination that attracted the Dutch seed company to provide long-term technical support for her business, leading to successful branding of her agricultural produce, which is a key for surviving in times of this crisis.

Hang did not have support from her family. Her Vietnamese friend in the USA taught her about coffee through online conversations. She was inspired by him and decided to try. She also reached out to another Vietnamese friend in Norway who produces organic fertilizers and imported them. She keeps learning about coffee online with other people who love coffee. During the interview, we were amazed by her in-depth knowledge about world coffee-tree varieties, and coffee beans and their differences in flavor. The fact that her enterprise and market were initiated from her social networks is a strength, especially during COVID-19, as her business is unaffected by global coffee markets.

Vietnamese people often believe entrepreneurs must have strong connections with politically and economically powerful people through families and relatives. Women's success in business is rarely viewed as arising from their own capacity, hard work, and effort but through their husbands' connections and financial support. The women in this chapter, however, show that passive connections given by family and relatives are not essential, but active connections developed by individual effort, interpersonal skills, and strong determination are. Longstanding cultivation of relationships helped these women to initiate and grow their enterprises, enabling them to navigate challenges during COVID-19.

Relationship of trust and worker well-being

Here, we move beyond the stories of COVID-19 and explore underlying business principles, which provide ideas of possible post-COVID-19 agribusiness models for women entrepreneurs. Agribusiness is often evaluated from an economic aspect, such as the scale of investment and production and number of employees. However, in this approach, those who use different criteria are under-evaluated. We now look at the three women's business principles.

Hang has three business principles: increasing coffee producers' value; reducing coffee waste by focusing on quality; and creating a business model of environmentally sustainable coffee production. She achieves this by building relationships of trust with her coffee producers with similar beliefs. She thinks that mass production and consumption of coffee typically undervalue and exploit producers, leaving them with high dependency on agricultural inputs and global coffee markets. In contrast, her business focuses on ensuring production quality depending on producers' quality of work and their faith. Relationships of trust is key for her business, both with producers and consumers.

Bich said that, at her age, she is not intending to earn more money or expand her business to increase profit. She is most proud that she employs ethnic minority people as workers on her farms as they tend to be poorer and marginalized compared to the ethnic majority. They no longer need to depend on forests as a source of income, which in turn contributes to forest conservation. Their children go to school and may even reach higher education, a transformative change. She is thinking of handing over her business to someone with a similar philosophy. She dreams before retiring to plant many flowering cherry trees in Lam Dong forests, indicating that her interests go far beyond securing personal profits and economic status.

"The profit is not for me. It's for my employees and for the society," Lan said immediately when we asked about her business goals. She prioritizes making her employees happy. She provides houses for her workers' families, offers loans for their children's university education, and organizes an annual company trip to a beach resort. Although some staff leave her employ to take their next career steps, she believes that investing in employees is key as they are assets of her company. She also keeps her company open to tourists, investors, and other entrepreneurs, providing space to share her experiences. As such, she gains trust from her employees, traders, and consumers.

The combination of economic savvy, close attention to building and maintaining social networks, and catering explicitly to worker well-being enabled them to survive during COVID-19, and even come out stronger for Lan. When we explore social, rather than economic, dimensions of agribusiness, the strengths of women's agribusiness in this crisis are illuminated.

Concluding remarks

This chapter illustrated the stories of three women agribusiness owners to understand social dimensions of entrepreneurship from women's perspectives. Feminist scholars point out that women entrepreneurs are often under-evaluated in male-orientated entrepreneur research as those studies tend to focus exclusively on quantity and economic aspects of entrepreneurship (Ahl, 2006; Hughes et al., 2012). Similarly, research on the impact of COVID-19 on agribusiness or agriculture tends to start from investigating economic impacts. The pandemic's economic impact is undeniable, and women entrepreneurs face many more challenges in this respect. However, women entrepreneurs have strengths in management and handling of business in times of crisis, in which their ethics, social values, and goals of agribusiness are vital.

Key characteristics of the women's agribusinesses we identified are social responsibility, open-mindedness, knowledge-sharing, environmental sustainability, a relationship of trust, informal networks, and online tools. While their businesses are global, their efforts are locally orientated, and their goals are associated with local, not global, stakeholders contributing to making their business resilient to the global crisis.

The pandemic, as an environmental and global problem, tells us that the globalization we have experienced in the past decades is fragile. The three women's approaches to agribusiness are alternative models to the profit-orientated capitalist economy, which are compatible with social and gender equality and environmental sustainability.

Acknowledgments

We thank the three women agribusiness owners for sharing their experiences. We are grateful to Cathy Farnworth and Paige Caroline Castellanos for their valuable comments on earlier drafts of this manuscript. This study was funded by CGIAR including the GENDER platform, the research program of Roots, Tubers and Bananas, and the research program of Policies, Institutions, and Markets led by the International Food Policy Research Institute. The opinions expressed here belong to the authors, and do not necessarily reflect those of CGIAR. This study was conducted within the Meryl Williams Fellowship program, funded by ACIAR.

Note

1 Names are changed to protect privacy.

References

Ahl, H. (2006). Why research on women entrepreneurs needs new directions. *Entrepreneurship Theory and Practice*, 30(5), 595–621.

Anh, P. (2020). 75,000 Vietnamese repatriated amid coronavirus pandemic. Available at: https://e.vnexpress.net/news/news/75-000-vietnamese-repatriated -amid-coronavirus-pandemic-4213029.html.

Hughes, K. D., Jennings, J. E., Brush, C., Carter, S., & Welter, F. (2012). Extending women's entrepreneurship research in new directions. *Entrepreneurship Theory and Practice*, 36(3), 429–442.

Nguyen, L. (2021). Hanoi's Covid-19 fight leaves street food vendors in the lurch [Online]. Available at: https://e.vnexpress.net/news/life/trend/hanoi-s-covid-19 -fight-leaves-street-food-vendors-in-the-lurch-4242668.html.

Stevano, S., Franz, T., Dafermos, Y., & Van Waeyenberge, E. (2021). COVID-19 and crises of capitalism: intensifying inequalities and global responses. *Canadian Journal of Development Studies/Revue canadienne d'études du développement*, 42(1-2), 1–17.

Worldometers. (2021). Covid live update [Online]. Available at: https://www .worldometers.info/coronavirus/ (Accessed March 24, 2021)

Part 2

Care work in families, households, and communities

5 COVID-19, gender, agriculture, and future research

Hannah Budge and Sally Shortall

Care work and COVID-19: stories from farming communities in Scotland

Coronavirus has undoubtedly impacted our global society in many unprecedented ways, affecting those from all walks of life. When we began to wonder about the consequences for women in the agriculture industry, we decided it would be best to hear from those who are involved in the sector. We conducted two focus groups with women in Scotland from a range of backgrounds who are connected to agriculture in various ways. Some are full-time farmers, some work part-time on the farm, some have senior positions off the farm but are involved in farming. We knew these women from previous research undertaken for the Scottish Government on women in agriculture in 2016 and 2017. Due to COVID-19, the focus groups were carried out by Zoom. Women from all over Scotland were involved in the Zooms, from the Scottish Borders with England right up to the Highlands. From the rich data, a number of themes emerged, and these are considered in turn. First, we examine what women described as the "reversal" of gender equality. Second, we consider the inequalities in domestic labor that became more pronounced during COVID-19. Finally, we look at the role women play as guardians of the mental well-being of their immediate and extended families. These discussions are followed by our reflections for future research.

"Reversal" of gender equality

All participants spoke of their frustrations of the immediate reversion to traditional gender roles in the household when lockdown began. One participant, a full-time farmer who suddenly found her husband and his employee working from home, commented that she felt there had been a regression

DOI: 10.4324/9781003198277-7

in her stance as a woman, and that effectively all the progression which had occurred throughout her lifetime was being taken away.

> I *regressed* to a woman's place, as in, you know, all the progress that I thought I had made in my life seemed to have slipped away.

This was due to being constantly expected to not just manage a farm, but to then take on the total management of the home with little help from partners and other household members. For instance, another commented that:

> I was the responsible functioning adult that had to cook and do the shopping and lamb ewes and calve cows ... And they're like looking at me waiting to be fed.

Another woman, who had a senior position off the farm, also felt there had been a reversal in the level of equality she thought she had earned:

> At home, I think people had got quite resilient because I'm not here that much. They had just gotten in their routine of just managing. Weirdly when I was here, they just expected me to just pick up and do every-thing. It felt like they *reverted* back to mum, mum will be in charge, mum will fix it.

In many respects, these quotes show the fragile nature of the gender equality that women have earned. Women have gained greater equality in the labor market. Yet this equality in paid employment, and increased participation in paid employment, has not translated into an equal division of domestic responsibilities. The European Institute for Gender Equality (2021) defines domestic responsibilities as "tasks performed inside a household in order to ensure that the basic needs of its members are met, such as cooking, cleaning, and taking care of children or older adults and other dependent family members." We are all aware that COVID-19 increased the amount of domestic responsibilities as adults worked from home, requiring addi-tional meals, and children were home schooled. It is to this we now turn (Figure 5.1).

COVID-19 and domestic responsibilities

With one exception, all women reported that while there were an increased number of adults in the house, the responsibility for cooking and cleaning fell to them. One farmer with two additional men home working reported:

Figure 5.1 Farmers in Shetland take a break during lambing time (Hannah Budge).

> I put a ready meal in the oven that nobody wanted to eat because they couldn't decide what they wanted to have, and then they wanted Yorkshire puddings with it. So in-between the ten minutes the Yorkshire puddings had to cook, I had to catch two ewes with mastitis. And they're *looking* at me waiting to be fed.

Prior to COVID-19 these men worked elsewhere and were responsible for their own lunch meals. Yet, the expectation that women provide the evening meal also spills into daytime even though women are also working full-time at home. Another woman, working full-time off the farm with children, said:

> He jumped in the machine and was off, I had to tell him to stop working because I can't do this. I can't be working my days and then have you coming home at half six, seven at night asking what's for tea and expecting me – and the kids coming through looking for tea as well.

This woman saw her husband as "jumping" into the tractor as a means of escape. He does contract work on other farms and she felt that this allows him to assume that all of the domestic responsibility falls to her because she is in the home, even though she is also working full-time and long days.

A woman who primarily does office work on the farm as well as part-time work in some organizations reported:

> I am going to sound like a broken record, obviously having to manage the childcare and home schooling, juggling that and then if the other person is committed to sort of twelve hours day, whether that be lambing, calving, sowing, whatever, just trying to juggle that, I think, puts extra pressure on the family and extra pressure I guess on relationships and everything else.

The key message is that when both partners are working full-time, domestic labor remains predominantly or solely women's work. This remained the case even when this work increased exponentially during COVID-19, underscoring the division of domestic labor as central to equality and well-being. Interestingly, we did find one exception. This was in an all-female household, where one woman farms full-time, her sister farms part-time, and now another sister and the mother are working from home during COVID-19. In this case, the women farmers were not expected to prepare meals. Rather the other two women working from home assumed this responsibility:

> Sometimes I will do it, sometimes it might be my Mum she might make it the night before. But it definitely wouldn't be Joan or Lori who are working on the farm.

It is interesting that here, where the non-farming household members are women, the women farmers are not expected to cook, which is different from previous participant's situation. It underlines the gendered understanding of expectations around domestic duties; women share domestic labor.

In all cases where women had children, they shouldered the weight of home schooling. There have been many newspaper reports regarding this issue; throughout COVID-19 it has consistently been the woman in the parenting partnership who is expected to take on the role of teacher, organize study time and when children do their homework. This was reflected by the women interviewed:

> It's the mum guilt. I feel that the home schooling landed on my plate to deal with. It didn't ever cross Ben's mind to enforce it. I felt it was me that had to engage with the school and find out what was happening. It was the whole guilt and it felt like I was still the one having to like to

make sure they still did physical activity like going for bike rides, and those kinds of things.

Women spoke about the additional burden of home schooling repeatedly, and also about feeling guilty that they were not achieving what they felt they ought to be. They worried their children were falling behind with their studies. In another case, one woman spoke about feeling she was failing because she compared herself to other mothers when her children reported progress to school and could see what other children had achieved:

> But that's all very well because their friends maybe have mums who are at home, or are furloughed,[1] who have got time and I think you get a bit of anxiety with that looking at what everybody is posting each day and interacting with the teachers. Whereas my pair are like … they've got so far behind that they're just not bothering, and it maybe slightly worries them a wee bit. It's not been great and I have felt very, very guilty not having time to sit with them.

Women presume that other women in families will carry the home-schooling responsibilities during COVID-19. These women judge themselves to have failed compared to other mothers who may have more time to invest in the process. Without exception the women in our focus groups with children shouldered this responsibility, even, in one case, involving three young children of different ages, and thus with different home-schooling needs (Figure 5.2).

Guardians of mental well-being during COVID-19

The focus group participants spoke about their different mental health responsibilities related to COVID-19. One woman involved with a mental health charity recounted that the number of women phoning for support on behalf of a male relative, and also wishing to know how they could best support them, had increased dramatically since the start of their pandemic. Others spoke of how women had felt they were responsible for the entire family:

> cooking, shopping, meds for elderly family, keeping the kids going, women are feeling that they're the ones responsible for keeping everything going and keeping everyone happy. Umm and that's a lot of pressure.

The pandemic has increased "mental" labor. There is providing support, but also ensuring routines, so that children maintain their mental well-being. Women reported this as exhausting:

Figure 5.2 Farmer using machinery to ready the hay (Hannah Budge).

> Mentally, my biggest issue has been headspace and it's going to sound, and I don't mean to sound kind of poor me, the cooking I don't mind but the having to make a decision every single day for what we are eating, what we are buying at the shops, what time the kids are getting out of bed, what we do during the day is overwhelming, on top of work.

Much of this mental labor is invisible. These are responsibilities that women largely do unspoken, in their heads. COVID-19 has increased the amount of this labor. As mentioned, the concern of the emotional well-being of others in the household falls again on the women in the household, one participant said:

> So yeah, so they are needing a hell of a lot of emotional support just now, and unsurprisingly that falls to me.

Mental health support also extends to the elderly and women spoke about how they also assumed responsibility for that. One woman said:

We are picking up the traditional role and caring of the elderly very much features in that. You want to look out for their mental health, I've got an eighty-year-old mother two miles up the road and the issue of isolation is very real.

While women spoke of their concerns about their children falling behind with schoolwork, they also talked about how their children's mental health and keeping them mentally well during the pandemic was a priority. They saw it as more important than schooling. This is clear from the following discussion in one of the focus groups:

Mary: People like me, people who are working on the farm that it's the home schooling that's gone. And we've had to say we cannot home school the kids. The kids are out with us, I actually think the kids, the kids look so bloody happy. They look happy, they look healthy, the do look really happy because they are together. You know we are just going to focus on the immediate, focus on the family, focus on matters for the next few months.

Harriet: My sister is a teacher, and their main thing is that they don't worry. About the education part of it, as long as children are happy that's the main thing, so you are right Mary.

Martha: We were very lucky in that Emma's teacher is very, very much your sister's thinking, Harriet, that you know, family and kind of being secure takes precedence.

The pandemic has highlighted the amount of mental labor that women do in the family, a form of labor we don't often think about, but which increased considerably during the pandemic. Women have increased the mental planning to do around more meals to be prepared, organizing daily routines for the family, organizing home schooling and combining this with their own work commitments. In addition, their role in ensuring the well-being of other family members is evident, ensuring they have support, company, and routines. This covers all generations, their spouses, children, and elderly parents. Women are ringing mental well-being helplines on behalf of their husbands, supporting children through home schooling, and missing friends, and ensuring elderly relatives stay connected and are not isolated. Particular issues arise for women caring for children on farms during the pandemic. The farm is a workplace as well as a home, and, as previous research has shown, it is a dangerous work place leading to increased stress of ensuring children are safely at play.

Reflections and future research

Disasters have often advanced women's equality. Both World Wars led to the increased participation of women in the labor market and undertaking farm work, which increased understanding of women's ability to contribute to productivity, to lead, and to make decisions. At this point in the pandemic, it seems to highlight the precarious nature of the equality women have achieved in the labor market. The focus has been on equality in the labor market and less on equality in the division of domestic labor. In terms of farming, we have tended to focus on how women secure entry to a masculine profession and how they are treated once they become farmers. In the future we will not just look at women's success in the industry as a measure of equality, we will also pay closer attention to the division of responsibilities within the home unit. Who has responsibility for what? We will also be mindful of the hidden mental domestic responsibilities; who organizes the day and who writes the grocery list are chores that often go unnoticed. Mental domestic labor is an area of research that requires much greater study. The most equal situation in the focus group was the farm where there are multiple women, some of whom do not work on the farm. We will question going forward whether, in agriculture, same-sex relationships and same-sex households have a fairer distribution of domestic labor and tasks.

Note

1   In the UK, the "furlough" scheme paid some workers unable to go to work while they were at home. It was a more generous payment than basic social security.

Reference

European Institute for Gender Equality. (2021) *Domestic responsibilities*. Available at https://eige.europa.eu/thesaurus/terms/1088 (Accessed 5 March, 2021).

6 Renegotiating care from the local to global

Kayla Yurco

The COVID-19 pandemic arrived as I was writing, among other life and work pursuits, from my home in Virginia about the ethics of care related to the gendered nature of livestock management in southern Kenya. An early career scholar – in 2020, in my third year as a tenure-track Assistant Professor – I was working on a manuscript based on my dissertation field-work from a few years ago, while also nodding toward research questions and plans anew for the next few years. As the pandemic escalated and my capacity to make space for writing unraveled, so too did my understanding of care in the unprecedented world that emerged: care for myself, care for my loved ones, care for my students and colleagues, and care for the communities I was writing about halfway across the world.

Care is central to my focus in several ways. One of my major projects over the last decade in Kenya aims to unveil the gendered nature of livestock management in pastoralist communities and demonstrate how collaborative or conflictual livestock caretaking activities influence gender roles. This work recognizes that the existing rich body of literature on human–livestock–environment interactions in sub-Saharan Africa has tended to focus primarily on herding activities in rangelands where livestock graze under the supervision of men. Pastoralist women's caretaking roles at home have often been overlooked, yet, as my research demonstrates, they are integral to decision-making about household economies.

The care work that pastoralist women do is so significant. I've found that gendered intra-household relations, rather than grazing activities or household assets like herd size, determine food security and coping/adaptive strategies: namely, availability of milk resources for individuals within households. Moreover, gender relations within pastoralist households are coproduced through milking practices that emerge as women exercise their responsibilities to apportion milk (to hungry calves and hungry children, husbands, guests, and for occasional sales) and as men attempt to preside over these activities (implementing, subverting, or affirming rules and

DOI: 10.4324/9781003198277-8

Figure 6.1 Morning milking events are important moments of care work (pre-
pandemic) (Kayla Yurco).

norms of use). Women are also the holders of ethnoveterinary knowledge:
with twice-daily milking activities, women physically connect with and
observe the health of cows in dynamic milking events (Figure 6.1). These
embodied moments of care inform women's difficult decisions about limited resources.

Through this care work, women navigate complex intra- and inter-
household dynamics associated with extended kin and, often, polygynous
families. Livestock-based resources, for example, are not divided equitably among women within households. And even though women "control"
milking activities, men control the allocation process of cattle to women.
The degree to which women access milk through those milking activities
is therefore influenced by the number of cows allocated to them, the number of dependents sharing resources, and the rigidity of rules associated
with milking events and milk use (Figure 6.2). Mixed-methods data from
hundreds of milking events and over 14 months of participant observation
demonstrate that men's behaviors of favoritism to different wives, efforts
by co-wives to cooperate or compete, and the extent of sharing for social
capital and coping strategies within and across households all factor in to
women's experiences of food security and well-being. Women hold great
autonomy in their roles as livestock caretakers but still must navigate com-
plicated household dynamics to enact that care.

Figure 6.2 A woman carries milk away from her household for sharing and selling
(pre-pandemic) (Kayla Yurco).

My findings align with efforts to expose the uncomfortable truth that
deep-rooted patriarchal traditions ingrained in resource management
practices in the Global South obscure the importance and complexity of
women's labor. More uncomfortable is the truth that patriarchal traditions
ingrained in academic discourse, theory, and methods also obscure the significance of women's labor. A clear example is the historical and normative
conceptual focus on the household as a unit of analysis in agrarian settings, a focus that translates to limited availability of empirical, gender-
disaggregated data from *within* households across the Global South. This
is true even as evidence mounts for how resource use, access, and management decisions are differentiated within households along gendered lines
worldwide.

The challenge here, and now more than ever, is that to understand gendered, embodied moments of care and their significance to women's lives,

we need to follow Joni Seager's (2014) call to "lift the roof off the house-hold" and see what makes a household work. Collecting gender-disaggre-gated data necessitates iterative feminist methodologies, collaboration with empowered research participants, and thoughtful reflections on positional-ity; i.e., it requires care. Practically, it also requires time actually spent *in* households. It requires so much time to understand the mundane, the ups and downs of the everyday, and the quirks that make us human – that which we might eventually codify as intra-household dynamics – time that allows us to process data points as characteristic of the collaborations and conflicts we all have across the proverbial dinner table.

Feminist methodologies, alongside a focus on ethics of care, have inspired new waves of gender-disaggregated research on intra-household dynamics. More and more studies, for example, point to the importance of women's care work as related to intra-household bargaining, negotiation, and patterns of decision-making for addressing social norms and structural inequities. Recognizing, valuing, and supporting care work seem critical for women's empowerment and intersectional food justice. As for my part in all of this: until last year, I've had the privilege to put my boots on the ground for a lot of time and often in my efforts to understand and write about these notions of care. Now, due to the global pandemic, I've had the privilege of wrestling with new notions of care from home. For instance: how can we keep caring and showing up for those we are writing about but cannot be with? And how can we care for ourselves in this uncertain era so that we can keep doing social and environmental justice work that empowers women in the gender–agriculture nexus now, and later?

Because there was, and is, much more to be done. While our momen-tum for this work has found a new obstacle in the arrival of the pandemic, what is more troubling are the ways that the pandemic amplifies preexisting gender inequities on communities, households, and individuals around the world.

Pastoralists and COVID-19

My field site in southern Kenya is just one of the many communities in the Global South where gender dynamics are coproduced with livestock man-agement. According to the International Livestock Research Institute, 1.3 billion people depend mainly on livestock for their livelihoods worldwide. And it is estimated that more than half of the world's pastoralists reside in increasingly contested drylands in sub-Saharan Africa. Traditional pastoral mobility has been based on seasonal risk management in drylands, and pas-toralists' short-term coping strategies and long-term adaptation strategies have been well studied across sub-Saharan Africa. Scholars of pastoralism have long understood the compound effects of climate change, policy shifts in land governance, and economic transitions that make pastoralists especially vulnerable in the modern world.

In reflecting on these vulnerabilities, some friends from southern Kenya have spoken of COVID-19 as a new, unprecedented threat; others have contextualized it as part of that compound threat. An important reality here is that pastoralism is predicated on movement and mobility – the very essence of what makes COVID-19 so challenging to control. It is no surprise that recent reports from across sub-Saharan Africa suggest that pandemic-related restrictions on movements exacerbated existing challenges for pastoralists. In the early months of the pandemic, for example, Ministry of Health guidelines in Kenya meant to curtail the spread of the virus resulted in the closure of open-air livestock markets and limits on gatherings of people. With livestock serving as a main store of wealth for most pastoralists, the closure of markets made it difficult to transpose those resources to cash for other household needs. In the meantime, livestock continued to breed and require movement and care.

And for pastoralists who have diversified livelihoods through involvement in small businesses, tourism, or conservation work – like those in my study site near the Maasai Mara National Reserve, where nearly every household has at least one member involved in one of those industries – the cessation of international flights, interruption of night-time travel, and closure of international borders amplified all of those challenges. As one of the premier wildlife safari destinations in East Africa (and as part of the tourism industry more broadly, an important contributor to Kenya's economy), this region felt the impacts of such closures strongly. Individuals and households who had responded to the last decade's challenges for a livestock-based economy (e.g., droughts, floods, and geopolitical tensions) by investing resources elsewhere struggled to move around to support their diversified household economies. Through all of this, labor burdens mounted, and dependence on livestock heightened.

But demands on labor have not been distributed equitably. A recent (2020) COVID-19 gender assessment report by UN Women confirms through countrywide surveys that women are disproportionately bearing pandemic-related burdens in Kenya, as is increasingly the case around the world. Early suspensions of movement affected the price and quantity of food supplies, straining women's responsibilities as provisioners of food. Nearly half of all households surveyed in Kenya reported a decline in food supplies in local markets and shops. Further, when schools were closed, families with children who relied on school feeding programs could no longer access these benefits; neither could they access education unless someone at home (often, women) could provide it. Given critical impacts of the pandemic on the informal sector where many women find wage work, more women lost their income than men. Women's access to sexual and reproductive healthcare has been impeded. And women have been pushed into more unpaid domestic and care work in their own homes and in those of family members and friends they support. Of course, the virus itself brought additional stressors to families with individuals who became ill or worse. The multilayered crisis is striking.

There are, however, a few bright spots. I'm learning from afar that the power of care work appears anew in a few places in southern Kenya's pastoralist communities, and elsewhere, and that adaptive efforts are already evident. Just as pastoralist women rely upon, and purposefully avoid, networks within and outside of their households for accessing livestock and milk, so too are they blurring public and private boundaries of households within their community in order to cope in the time of COVID-19. Care efforts are manifesting strongly at the community level. Women's groups – long recognized for providing a safe physical, emotional, and financial haven for women in times of conflict and hardship and in times of celebration and joy – remain vital during the pandemic. Participation there requires care work, too, but these groups materialize the kind of care for one another that, interestingly, works as a respite from the demands of everyday care at home.

Care work has been innovative in other spaces, too. Local conservancy associations are partnering with non-profit groups for recovery planning, working to ensure the longevity of a conservation land-leasing model that hopes to continue to support diversified local livelihoods in the region well into the future. Elsewhere in Kenya, new alliances of self-organizing community groups function as liaisons with local government officials to disseminate and share pandemic-related information. Telecommunications systems are being fast-tracked for veterinarians and livestock experts to provide advice for small-scale livestock-holders over mobile phones. While these tools are certainly useful in a time of social distancing and limited mobility, this mode of care work has real promise for the future. These systems have scalable impacts beyond COVID for pastoralists to manage day-to-day animal health challenges while balancing other familial and diversified professional responsibilities. Importantly, there is also the potential for these systems to help control future escalations of animal disease.

Care ethics from and at home

For now, I'm learning about these moments of harm and hope from afar. It's already the case that COVID-19 has ushered in significant efforts toward care-related research in the virtual sphere, with great emphasis on remote methodologies. Discussions are trending toward a reconceptualized ethics of care in scholarship and practice as we cope with the challenges of engaged, collaborative, and participatory partnerships in the time of crisis, often remotely. These discussions are difficult but remind me of the value of a gender transformative approach: it is adaptive and responsive. There is real resilience in the power of care.

As such, lately, I've felt that a focus on care, and the resilience it offers, might help us communicate and position these personal-political overlaps in this unprecedented complexity of care needs. This is about confronting individual privileges inherent in admitting how challenging it is to work on these topics during this difficult time while continuing to forge forward anew. Closer to home, I see (and feel) the everyday burdens on faculty continuing to mount. My care work involves a measured embrace of my own pandemic-related stresses and losses while still trying to show up as best I can for others I care so deeply about, locally and across the globe, and *their* stresses and losses. I see the need for *recognizing* care work everywhere, and I see the need for more care work everywhere, too.

Honest reflections on the power of care – the vulnerability of needing, expressing, and giving it – as individuals might give us the means to keep offering it toward our local, national, and global communities in this extraordinary time. Embracing the dynamic nature of care at a variety of scales might help us keep harnessing it toward ally-ship, organizing, action, and all else that is needed, especially to those experiencing heightened inequities in the agri-food system due to legacies of systemic marginalization, oppression, and violence.

Pre-pandemic, I didn't imagine that these questions of care would become the centralizing focus of my day-to-day energies. But care looks really different to me now. Many days, I try to hold space for care in discussions that pan out over text with the friends, colleagues, and research participants in Kenya who have made my career possible. COVID-19 has impacted their lives in ways I can only begin to understand from afar and has brought unprecedented challenges to their caretaking activities. Closer to home, a lot of my energy goes to holding space for local and community caretaking while asking difficult questions about my loved ones (e.g., is it care to visit my parents, or is it care to *not* visit them?). And with the fourth semester of teaching in the time of COVID looming ahead, my work now includes regular readings on the ethics of care in trauma-informed pedagogy and focused preparation to encourage self-care practices for my students in, and outside, the (virtual/hybrid/online) classroom. It is less clear to me to what degree this work manifests as care for my students or as self-care.

What is clear to me is that there is so much care work to be done. I'm aiming to contribute to the complexity, in part, by holding an honest space to reimagine and renegotiate my sense of, capacity for, and commitment to, care. I'm warmly looking to learn from others struggling and succeeding with the same.

References

Seager, J. 2014. *Background and Methodology for Gender Global Environmental Outlook.* Nairobi, Kenya: United Nations Environment Programme.

UN Women-Kenya. 2020. *COVID-19 Gender Assessment: Gender Perspective Kenya.* Available at https://data.unwomen.org/publications/covid-19-gender -assessment-kenya.

Part 3

Intersectional inequalities in the food system

7 Facing COVID-19 in rural Honduras: experiences of an indigenous women's association

Alfredo Reyes, Hazel Velasco, Mercedes García, and Olga Pérez

Positionality

Given current events, and as Central American researchers, we are committed to highlighting the impacts of the COVID-19 pandemic in our region, especially in those communities that were already in a vulnerable situation as a result of the economic and social inequities that characterize our countries. After working for almost six years in the rural areas of western Honduras, mainly with the Lenca ethnic communities and specifically with women farmers, one of our first thoughts was: how will the pandemic impact those smallholders' livelihoods?

In this chapter, we seek to present the experiences, struggles, and tactics of Lenca women to cope with the pandemic's effects. At the same time, Alfredo and Hazel recognize their limitations by not being part of these communities and being currently outside the region. Therefore, we decided to write together with the Association of Renewed Intibucan Women (AMIR) to develop a narrative that prioritizes their voices, experiences, and perceptions. AMIR is a grassroots association of indigenous Lenca women that possesses a long history of advocacy for women's rights throughout the communities of the municipality of Intibucá in Honduras. Thus, the members of this organization hold the insiders' knowledge to understand the struggles faced and strategies implemented by their members throughout the pandemic.

A pre-COVID-19 glance at the smallholders' horticultural producers in rural Honduras

The communities in western Honduras rely on agriculture and their harvests' commercialization in the surrounding urban areas as their main livelihood.

DOI: 10.4324/9781003198277-10

In the case of the Lenca populations that inhabit the department of Intibucá, their products consist mainly of fruit and vegetables, which are quickly perishable. Also, the communities lack adequate storage infrastructure, and in some cases, no electricity is available to maintain the cold chain needed to extend the crops' lives. These challenges force smallholder farmers to transport their products to the sale sites as soon as possible. Most households in the area are small vegetable producers who typically lack formal safety nets, such as agricultural insurance or access to emergency funds (Sanders, 2019), which significantly limits their ability to respond to external shocks, such as a pandemic. Additionally, traditional gender roles in the region limit women's ability to acquire and control productive assets or access formal financial services and education (Larson, Castellanos, and Jensen, 2019). These factors impact their bargaining power within the household, which leaves them even more vulnerable to potential crises.

In general terms, vegetable marketing in the Intibucá is carried out in three main ways. The best quality vegetables are commercialized either through producers' associations or through intermediaries; in both instances, the product is distributed to supermarkets in the country's main cities. Men usually receive the payment for those sales, and, therefore, they decide on the destination of that income. On the other hand, lower-quality vegetables are sold in local markets, and women are usually responsible for those sales and are the ones who determine what to do with that income.

The Lencas and *Asociación de Mujeres Intibucanas Renovadas* (AMIR)

The Lencas are the largest indigenous group in Honduras, comprising 63 percent of total ethnic groups and 6 percent of the Honduran population (INE, 2013). Their distribution is concentrated in western Honduras, where more than 90 percent of the Lenca population live in the Departments of Intibucá, La Paz, and Lempira (INE, 2013). In the areas where the Lencas are found, rural and indigenous populations suffer alarming levels of poverty and malnutrition. Moreover, 72 percent of indigenous households, compared to 41.6 percent of households nationwide, cannot cover the basic food-basket costs, which places them on the extreme poverty line (CADPI, 2017). Due to the adverse socioeconomic conditions indigenous communities face, western Honduras has become a focus of international development organizations during the last 20 years. The efforts to support these populations have focused on shifting their production systems by integrating more efficient practices and introducing high-value crops like horticulture or coffee. Thus, development agencies have reinforced this strategy as a means to fight poverty and food insecurity levels in the area.

In this context, AMIR emerged in 1980 as an indigenous women's grass-roots organization focused on improving its members' and families' lives. The organization started focusing on human rights and empowerment but has expanded to other topics including food security, sustainable agriculture, and food processing. At present, AMIR has an active membership of about 450 women distributed across 28 community-based groups. They provide their members' technical assistance in maize, beans, fruits, and vegetables. AMIR members are also trained to establish home gardens and food processing (Figure 7.1), and they can request loans to establish productive crops such as strawberries and potatoes.

Figure 7.1 Prior to the COVID-19 pandemic, AMIR members participate in a Farmer Field School about biointensive home gardens[1] in the community of Malguara, Intibucá, Honduras (Alfredo Reyes).

AMIR also has a processing plant that receives and purchases its members' fruit to transform it into wines, sweets, jams, and preserves. The plant has functioned as a mechanism to ensure the sale of women's products and provide them with an income option within their households. AMIR products are sold locally under the "Siguatas Lencas" brand.

National and local context during the pandemic

In the next section, we take a look at the short-term direct and indirect effects that the COVID-19 pandemic had on the Lenca communities served by AMIR. Additionally, we cover the events one year after the pandemic first entered Honduras and the combined effects of the Eta and Iota hurricanes.

On March 16, 2020, with eight confirmed cases of COVID-19 in the country, the government of Honduras issued the first statement restricting the movement of people and requested the indefinite closure of non-essential businesses nationwide (UNAH, 2020). Local government relied on the military and the police to enforce the measures and deployed agents on the main highways, to deter and arrest offenders.

In parallel, at a community level, residents in Intibucá rural areas established *mesas de seguridad* (security councils), which regulated neighbors' movement and although they did not have the power to penalize those who did not comply with the community quarantine, they were supported by the police to enforce the law. Besides, the few COVID-19 reported cases in the rural communities of Intibucá were linked to intermediaries moving agricultural products to the cities. This narrative reinforced the urgency to stop all types of mobility and led to the blockade of roads for almost two months.

The state of Honduras enforced restrictive mobilization measures, and their severity changed as the COVID-19 cases increased or decreased. In this way, when a decrease in infections was reported, the measures were relaxed, and when the cases were increasing, the restriction measures were reestablished. The state of Honduras used the license plates and personal identification numbers to limit the number of people circulating in public spaces. The measure that persisted without distinction between urban and rural areas was controlling the circulation of citizens through their identification card number, allowing people to leave their homes every 15 days for personal chores, such as grocery shopping or banking.

Most of these restrictive measures were lifted when two consecutive Hurricanes hit Honduras. First Eta, a Category 4 hurricane, entered Honduran territory on November 3, 2020, followed two weeks later by Iota, a Category 5 hurricane. In Honduras, the negative impacts of both hurricanes mostly occurred along the north coast. The floodwaters inundated wide areas of northern Honduras, including entire communities

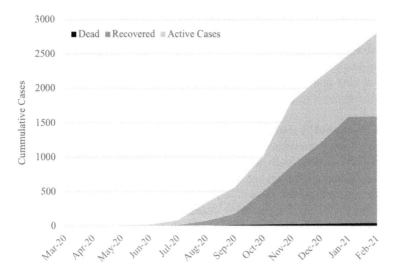

Figure 7.2 COVID-19 Cumulative cases in Intibuca, Honduras (Sinager, 2021).

and San Pedro Sula International Airport. Nonetheless, the continuous rain from both storms affected the electricity service, roads, and crops nationwide.

To date, the number of COVID-19 cases in the Department of Intibucá has increased (Figure 7.2), with the vast majority reported as occurring in urban areas. However, when compared with the rest of the country the number has remained low, with 1,433 active cases reported by February 2021. The evidence of COVID-19 cases in the rural areas of Intibucá is mainly anecdotal, such as when a relative in severe health conditions must be transported to be treated at the public hospital at la Esperanza Town.

The short-term effects of the COVID-19 pandemic on agriculture and rural women

The consequences of the movement restrictions on the agricultural sector were evident almost immediately. For example, during the first months of quarantine, households were unable to sell their products outside the community, which significantly reduced their incomes. Many smallholders lost most of the harvest, especially those households dedicated to the production of vegetables and potatoes. Regarding these events, one of AMIR members explained that:

The quarantine has affected us severely because we hoped to sell our vegetables, and we could not. Many families invested and took out loans but could not generate income. We were unable to sell most of the harvest, and even what we sold was not at the expected price. The biggest problem now is that people have run out of working capital. In this new planting cycle, we see more corn being planted because the investment is low.

Furthermore, AMIR members have expressed that, although intermediaries can now transit between communities, households do not have products to sell because they were unable to replant their fields or to provide the required quantities. Moreover, the Honduran government announces and extends the containment measures weekly, which gives producers insufficient time for planning and seeking alternatives.

In the case of women, the pandemic has made it impossible for them to mobilize to sell their products in the city of La Esperanza. As previously mentioned, this marketing channel has been essential for women in the area and their ability to generate income. Additionally, in the case of AMIR members, the restrictions coincided with the highest fruit-production period. In previous years, AMIR trained and supported its members on the establishment of fruit crops such as peaches, strawberries, and blackberries that are bought by AMIR's processing plant to be transformed into wines, jams, and sweets. The income generated by these sales have become relevant for AMIR members' livelihoods.

Strategies implemented by AMIR and its members

To face the new economic difficulties in the face of COVID-19 in combination with government measures, AMIR members have used different strategies. At the community level, women have organized to sell and exchange available crops and products:

> People who had vegetables exchanged with those who had cheese or eggs. Inside the communities, neighbors started to move the products as they were needed; the groceries that usually came from the city became scarce. For example, the stores ran out of bakery products, and women started making bread to sell, and that is how they are finding other options.

Moreover, AMIR members who had established home gardens had a variety of crops to meet household needs and, in some cases, they were able to sell or trade with their neighbors. For AMIR's staff, the pandemic represents an

Figure 7.3 AMIR delivers food and cleaning kits in the community of Planes Río
Grande, Intibucá, Honduras (AMIR).

event that can strengthen their connections with international cooperation
and an opportunity to seek projects that can benefit their members. As part
of their actions, AMIR negotiated a new project with OXFAM Honduras
and was also able to reallocate funds from an existing initiative with the
Inter-American Foundation. These initiatives have allowed them to deliver
food and cleaning kits to 436 households (each kit valued at 1,000 lempiras
or approximately USD 40) and 1,000 lempiras cash bonuses to 400 members. The delivery of the bonuses in the form of cash was an essential decision since it considers that each woman has different needs. AMIR currently
has 450 active members (Figure 7.3).

AMIR staff resumed their activities and field visits by June 2020. They
have used WhatsApp and "short message service" (SMS) as their main
communication channel to organize workshops. During their field visits,
they work with small groups in open spaces to keep their members safe.
They have tried delivering workshops via Zoom, but insufficient connection
in rural areas has rendered this option ineffective (Figure 7.4).

One year and two hurricanes

After a year of living with the pandemic, maintaining the security measures has become a daily challenge for the Lenca communities. As presented
in the previous section, the pandemic's initial effects directly affected the

Figure 7.4 AMIR delivers cleaning kits and cash bonuses in the communities, Intibucá, Honduras (AMIR).

commercialization of agricultural products from rural areas to urban centers. As mobility restrictions were lifted, those who had products available continued to be affected by transportation availability. When transportation was restored, the mayor's office tried to limit passenger numbers within the transportation units, which was not a sustainable option for either the bus owners nor their passengers. The buses started to run at full capacity, thus limiting the space available to transport agricultural products.

During this time, AMIR focused on providing biosafety kits that include masks and alcohol gel, but not in the capacity to supply all its members and their families. In this sense, an AMIR member mentioned that:

> For us, it is costly to be buying masks when we have to cover other needs. When we travel on the buses, we reuse the masks that AMIR has given us, but not all people have the means to wear face protection or follow all the security measures.

Traveling to urban areas is still a necessity that people cannot avoid as it continues to be the main market for agricultural products and the only place where they can get inputs for their production. The consecutive arrival of Hurricanes Eta and Iota at the end of 2020 increased the difficulties experienced in the area due to the pandemic. The communities of Río Grande, Mixcure, Azacualpita, Yamaranguila, and Belén were among the most affected. Once again, transport between rural communities and the urban area was interrupted by landslides that blocked the roads.

On the other hand, the communities were preparing for the harvest of second-season corn and beans. An AMIR member reported that:

> We had already folded the corn and were waiting for it to finish drying to start the harvest. That is when the rain came that did not stop for several days, the corn was *nacido* (covered with fungi), and we lost the entire harvest. Due to the amount of water, the beans were also ruined.

Intercropping corn and beans is part of AMIR's initiative to rescue indigenous cultivation practices and strengthen its members' food security. The initiative was accompanied by a seed bank and grain storage to be created with the harvest. In addition to corn, AMIR members lost their vegetable crops and fruit that were part of the home garden program that the association has been promoting.

After the hurricanes impacted the area, AMIR staff changed its role into delivering humanitarian aid. They visited the most affected communities to deliver food, biosafety, and hygiene equipment, blankets, and clothing for women and girls. AMIR has focused on capitalizing on its network with international NGOs to access new projects and funding to support their members. Based on last year's experiences, they shifted their approach to strengthening their members' resiliency by focusing on the development of a revolving fund, the establishment of irrigation systems and home gardens, the rescue of the *milpa*, support of entrepreneurship initiatives, the acquisition of land for collective use, and the creation of a seed and grain bank.

Future considerations

It is difficult to predict the pandemic's long-term impacts on Lenca women and their households. Although the restriction measures have been effective in avoiding contagion in the area, they have jeopardized the sustainablilty of small producers' livelihoods.

In terms of the immediate effects, we have evidenced drastic changes in the preferred crop choices. Households have increased planting corn and beans since they require low investment and are easy to store; however, they have low economic value. The transition to basic grains and monoculture can harm households by reducing their income. Nonetheless, in the long term, these changes can have a profound impact by limiting the diversity of available agricultural products in the communities and increasing their vulnerability to other threats such as climate change.

Furthermore, it will also be necessary to explore how these decisions are made within households and how women's positions and power in the household will be impacted, particularly after evidencing how their income sources have been affected. Additionally, in the face of external shocks, evidence suggests that women's assets, such as small farm animals, are the first to be liquidated (Quisumbing, Kumar, and Behrman, 2018).

Although AMIR members expressed concern about the future and the evident reduction of income in their households, they also consider that the restrictive measures have been necessary:

> We are here [in the community] because we are afraid of getting sick, not because we have been locked up. We prefer to stay at home, even if we lack something, instead of going out and risking getting sick or making our family sick.

Note

1   The WAgN: Honduras project included a research and extension team from the Pennsylvania State University and Zamorano University, with funding from USAID's Feed the Future Horticulture Innovation Lab at UC Davis, and partnered with AMIR to implement gender-integrated Farmer Field Schools.

References

CADPI (2017) *Nota ténica de país sobre cuestiones de los pueblos indígenas: República de Honduras.*

Instituto Nacional de Estadísticas (2013) *Censo: XVII Censo de Población y VI de Vivienda.* Tegucigalpa, Honduras.

Larson, J. B., Castellanos, P. and Jensen, L. (2019) 'Gender, household food security, and dietary diversity in western Honduras', *Global Food Security*, 20, pp. 170–179. doi:10.1016/j.gfs.2019.01.005.

Quisumbing, A. R., Kumar, N. and Behrman, J. A. (2018) 'Do shocks affect men's and women's assets differently? Evidence from Bangladesh and Uganda', *Development Policy Review*, 36(1), pp. 3–34. doi:10.1111/dpr.12235.

Sanders, A. (2019) *Assembling the Horticulture Value Chain in Western Honduras.* Penn State University.

SINAGER (2021) *Coronavirus COVID-19 En Honduras.* Available at: https://covid19honduras.org/ (Accessed: March 8, 2021).

UNAH (2020) *Cronología de la pandemia Covid 19 en Honduras.* Available at: https://mdd.unah.edu.hn/publicaciones/cronologia-de-la-pandemia-covid-19-en-honduras (Accessed: August 3, 2020).

8 Cultivating community resilience: working in solidarity in and beyond crisis

Angie Carter

I live in Michigan's Upper Peninsula on the shores of Lake Superior, and so I waited until mid-March 2020 to start my tomato seeds and the beginnings of the garden I would plant in early summer. As other gardeners can tell you, it is easy to start too many; the seeds are so small and there are so many contingencies. What if some of the seeds don't germinate, or the soil gets a fungus, or the plants are damaged in the process of repotting and replanting? I didn't yet know that I'd share these extra plants among friends, neighbors, and students as they, too, started gardens, many for the first time.

As I tended these seeds, cities and states in the United States initiated voluntary and mandatory stay-at-home orders in response to COVID-19. Soon after, stories about food supply chain fears and the unsafe working conditions of food laborers filled the news. Grocery store shelves emptied. Families lost childcare, jobs, and, in too many cases, lives.

In the spring of 2020, Women, Food and Agriculture Network (WFAN) began to virtually organize members in response to the developing crisis. In addition to being a gardener, I am also a rural sociologist studying agriculture and food. My work is informed through my relationships within the Women, Food and Agriculture Network (WFAN), a 501(c)(3) non-profit organization with a mission "to engage women in building an ecological and just food and agricultural system through individual and community power" (WFAN, n.d.). I also serve on WFAN's board. WFAN began as, and remains, the only national sustainable agricultural non-profit organization organized by and for those identifying as women and as non-binary. Started in Iowa in the mid-1990s, the organization now has national reach and includes those working in sustainable agriculture, food systems, food justice, and community health and nutrition.

WFAN's COVID-19 organizing began by emphasizing "community-centered tools which are significant in ensuring that community health is a critical priority, not just now, but always," as described by staff member Amy Kousch in WFAN's Profiles in Resilience (Kousch, 2020). Then-staff-member

DOI: 10.4324/9781003198277-11

Moselle Singh invited WFAN members to join a virtual discussion about localized mutual aid efforts and encouraging knowledge-sharing across the network. Together, staff members Kousch, Singh, and Almitra began what would become known as WFAN's Growing Community Resilience program.

I took part in these calls, adding updates to shared spreadsheets and reporting from my own community. The discussions, initially held weekly, evolved in their format from free-form forums to inviting members to volunteer to share more specific examples of grassroots community collaboration. For example, board member Sarah Carroll shared her efforts to organize mutual aid by knocking on doors within her Minneapolis neighborhood: "It has been heartwarming and securing to know that we actually have many of the resources we need right here in our neighborhood" (WFAN, 2020a). The early calls lasted a couple hours each, as we compared notes on what was happening where we lived and created a space of care and support despite the escalation of cases reported each day in the news. This was needed space to share strategies and resources as we worked through the beginnings of a global pandemic event many of us continue to experience in isolation.

In late April, WFAN's Kousch (2020) had written the following in a blog about the Growing Community Resilience meetings:

> I think our power in adapting, despite harm, for generations, is serving us during our current public health pandemic and paradigm of trauma – and perhaps in ways that we might not readily name. I suspect, though it is far too early to make any prediction, but my guess is that when we collectively begin to sift through the processes that authentically serve communities in an equitable way, we will find that these undervalued tools of listening to hear, acting with understanding, and creating intentional spaces of discourse – these tools that are often forged by trauma (whether individual or collective), resilience and vulnerability – these will be the tools that we will critically rely on to rebuild from a wellspring of respect for living systems.

Her words foretold a year in which the shared violence of the pandemic and white supremacy would push us to hone those tools.

In late May, I finally planted my tomato plants just as protests and vigils began to fill our communities. That same week, a police officer in Minneapolis killed George Floyd over an alleged counterfeit US$20 bill; the tragedy brought renewed attention to the murders of Ahmaud Arbery and Breonna Taylor earlier that spring. WFAN's Growing Community Resilience meetings refocused to identify how the pandemic's food crisis intersected with our nation's racial justice crisis, and what WFAN members could do to educate themselves and take action on both fronts. Soon after, WFAN shared a Statement in Solidarity with the Movement for Black Lives (WFAN, 2020b), collaboratively written by staff and board members to acknowledge WFAN's position as a majority-white agricultural organization in a food system rooted in Indigenous genocide, enslaved labor of African Americans, and the continuous exploitation of BIPOC (Black, Indigenous, people of color). In the statement, WFAN committed to prioritizing anti-racism and challenging members through shared learning and hard conversations not only about the patriarchal control of resources and land in agriculture, but white settler control. At the same time, WFAN as an organization matched the financial contributions of WFAN board and staff members to BIPOC-led food and agriculture groups.

As WFAN organized the Growing Community Resilience across the national network, I organized locally with community partners where I live. I had planned to spend the summer engaging in community-based research with the Western UP Food Systems Council (WUPFSC), studying our regional food systems knowledge-exchange networks and planning feasibility studies for future collaborative infrastructure through interviews and listening circles. The pandemic shifted our plans as project partners and I did not want to place more burden than was already mounting upon our communities during the pandemic.

Quickly, we pivoted from planning interviews and listening circles to creating biweekly virtual grower meet-ups and a listserv for farmers' markets, farmers, and community gardeners to share information and questions about what the summer season would look like, resources needed, and how to move forward. What did our community gardens need to organize for the coming season? Where could people find seed, soil? Should the farmers plant planning for the summer farmers' markets to still take place? How would we support those most vulnerable in our community, for whom food is already difficult to access even in non-pandemic times? Since our season starts so late, we had the advantage of time on our side to learn from others downstate and across the country who were already actively coordinating gardens and farmers' markets. We were also lucky that we'd already been organizing locally over the past two years as a grassroots group of local farmers, gardeners, teachers, food advocates, planners, public health representatives, and members of the Keweenaw Bay Indian Community's Natural Resource Department.

WUPFSC's is located within a region of Ojibwe homelands and territory extending into northern Wisconsin; that I have the privilege as a white settler descendant to work and live on these lands was made possible through the Treaty of 1842 between the United States and the nations of Keweenaw Bay, Lac Vieux Desert, La Courte Oreilles, Lac Du Flambeau, Red Cliff, St. Croix, and Sokaogon Mole Lake. The Keweenaw Bay Indian Community and Lac Vieux Desert Band of Lake Superior Chippewa, both located within the contemporary boundaries of the Western UP, lead and inform different parts of the WUPFSC's efforts, sharing teachings, and building community through food sovereignty events and other opportunities to learn from our more-than-human relatives what it means to take care of our shared home.

The Great Lakes region is a place of food abundance. Wild and foraged foods and medicines, gardens, fish; the gifts of these lands and waters have fed people since time immemorial. And yet, the copper boom and subsequent deindustrialization of these lands, along with the continued contamination of its waters, has resulted in high rates of economic instability and food insecurity. Informal food exchange in the UP, including gifting and bartering, are important, though often devalued, forms of food access among both the Ojibwe and the immigrant/settler descendants. We centered these traditions in our local food organizing in response to the pandemic. Our organizing intentionally worked to avoid the stigmatization of poverty, insisting upon fresh food as a right and emphasizing reciprocity and mutuality, as shared through the teachings of Keweenaw Bay Indian Community Natural Resource Department collaborators.

An emergent group from WUPFSC started a program they named "Growing from the Heart," to remove the stigma from food assistance in this time of crisis by inviting anyone from our communities to grow and safely share fresh produce with our neighbors via existing food service programs, pantries, and front-porch steps (WUPFSC, n.d.). Students involved in this effort started a student-run collective growing gifted seeds and plant starts on three different private properties. Members of this Down to Earth Garden Collective included LGBTQIA and BIPOC students for whom gardening was new; together they prioritized food sovereignty as a form of healing with one another and the Earth. Their leadership in our now-virtual food systems organizing pushed WUPFSC to more intentionally acknowledge not only settler colonialism but also anti-Black racism in our communities.

In the summer of 2020, as we began to try to navigate what the pandemic would mean for our communities, we also began to incorporate discussions about racial equity within our WUPFSC meetings. We'd taken for granted that because our group was comprised of Ojibwe and white settler descendant members that we must already be paying attention to race; we learned, though, that we were not being intentional about (un)learning the ways in which anti-Black racism shaped our food system. We began and continue to discuss together what it means to engage in food-systems work on treaty lands and in this acute moment of crises; to this end, we have devoted part of our biweekly planning meetings to collaborative learning, our members rotating to lead different discussions or reflective activities about power and justice.

WFAN's Growing Community Resilience meetings transitioned to take place biweekly and then monthly; their format evolved, too, moving to a more structured space including prompts and readings to inform collective discussions. The meetings began to break out into caucus or affinity groups for a good portion of the time together, white folks meeting with white folks and BIPOC folks meeting with BIPOC folks in Zoom break-out rooms. The purpose of these spaces was to intentionally cultivate communities of support and also actively engage white people in critical examination of how whiteness and gender have worked together to maintain the status quo in agriculture and food systems. As a white woman, I attended the white caucus groups, and often volunteered as a board member to facilitate one of the white caucus break-outs. After intentional discussion in our caucus groups, we would rejoin at the end of the meetings with the other groups to debrief together.

Offline and in safely-masked distanced communion with members of my community, I took to the streets of my small town as so many did across the country and globe. In addition to marches, I joined one of my departmental colleagues in a weekly vigil on the bridge downtown to hold signs for justice for Breonna Taylor and George Floyd. The students from the Down to Earth Garden Collective joined her, too, and so the vigil for racial justice became a part of the tending to the gardens, a place and space both to bear witness in our majority-white community to the continued harm of white supremacy and to organize resistance as we worked together to feed our neighbors.

As we know too well, there is so much work to do – even among those already committed to food justice and equity in agriculture – to connect how our relationships with the land are mirrored in our relationships with each other. The continued police brutality targeting Black lives and the health inequities exacerbated by COVID-19 are preexisting conditions of our larger economic system. Similarly, the recklessness of Tyson, Smithfield, and other agrifood corporations in failing to protect their workers during this global pandemic are externalized costs in a system of food production and national food policy that prioritizes cheap food and commodifies the lives of agricultural and food laborers (Davis 2020; Douglas 2020; Valdivia 2020). This continued violence is not accidental, but the outcome of hundreds of years of white supremacy created to power capitalist expansion; first through plantations and now through corporations.

Monica White's (2018) *Freedom Farmers: Agricultural Resilience and the Black Freedom Movement* analyzes how Black agrarianism has created, and continues to create, alternative systems and community transformation. White writes:

> Community resilience is a way for a community to absorb a disturbance and reorganize itself while undergoing change. White resilience

as a concept often does not take into account structural approaches and community engagement that includes indigenous knowledge and emotional experiences, and the kind of interracial and intraracial exchanges that we need to adapt.

(145)

Across the country, in cities and in rural communities, people are calling attention to the consequences of white resiliency and pushing for accountability and change. The WFAN staff had not read White's work when they first began to facilitating the "Growing Community Resilience" efforts ("it's on order!" one shared with me when I asked), yet their organizing aligns with White's call for structural change, critical reflection, and community engagement, as well as valuation of the knowledges already held among the many diverse members of our communities, in the shared work toward transformation. White's emphasis on interracial and intraracial exchange, as well as WFAN board member Sarah Carroll's point that the resources and knowledge we need to attend to these crises are "right here," in our own communities, empowers and compels us to begin the hard work of transformation now as we learn from and care for each other.

WUPFSC's plans for the summer of 2021 look a lot like they did last summer; the virtual planning is already underway. The programs we started a year ago will continue and, hopefully, grow stronger. In our own local food organizing in the western Upper Peninsula, even across Indigenous-settler community divides, the pandemic highlighted the work we must do to begin to dismantle the ways white supremacy shapes our collaborations.

WFAN's Growing Community Resilience calls have been underway for one year and now take place monthly. Attendees shift from month to month, though some attend every meeting. In late February 2021, I helped to facilitate an affinity group discussion with other white women about our connections to land, engaging in a reflective exercise in which each of us examined how our race/ethnicity, gender identity and expression, sexuality, and access to healthcare, education, and networks influenced our connections and/or access to land. We discussed the Justice for Black Farmers Act and how to develop understanding for and support of reparations in our communities. I remain humbled and inspired by the depth of engagement possible with people previously strangers who are similarly committed to change and are in different places in the work of organizing in and with their communities. WFAN is working now to integrate these critical conversations about whiteness, power, and racial justice underway in the Growing Community Resilience program across all its programming.

It is now March 2021 and we are a year into the pandemic. I have three jars left of the tomatoes I canned from my garden last year; time capsules of a summer of uncertainty and grief, but also of sunshine and long days here in the north woods and the energy of that summer spent organizing locally through WUPFSC and remotely through WFAN. The headlines this week bring stories about accelerated vaccine production as well as photos of the concrete barriers and barbed wire erected by the City of Minneapolis around the courthouse where, later this month, a jury will sit to listen to the opening statements of the former Minneapolis police officer charged in George Floyd's murder. Meanwhile, across the world, some 250 million farmers and rural people in India are organizing the largest ongoing protest demanding the repeal of three Farm Acts passed by the Parliament of India in 2020. Agricultural organizations, such as WFAN, that released statements in solidarity with BLM, now are posting statements in solidarity with India's farmers and rural people. As we engage more deeply in our own neighborhoods, so too must we connect across movements and geographies, and keep pushing our networks and organizations to provide not just words but real change in the work we say and do support. Some of us, especially white folks, have had a crash course in community care; it is time to reorient and recommit our work for the long term.

"The pandemic is a portal," Arundhati Roy wrote presciently in her April 2020 essay of the same name; "it offers us a chance to rethink the doomsday machine we have built for ourselves." We've been in pandemic mode now for a year in the United States, and working our way through and out of white supremacist mode now for more than 245 years; and yet, as Kousch reminds us, the tools we forge through trauma are powerful testament to our individual and collective power. At local and national levels, our networks engage in critical examination, reflection, and interracial and intraracial exchanges described in White's conceptualization of community resilience as necessary in the formation of a prefigurative politics and transformation. We are, as individuals and as collectives, remembering and recommitting to transformative acts of care for ourselves and others that will, eventually, dismantle the machine.

References

Douglas, L. 2020, 'Mapping COVID-19 Outbreaks in the Food System', *Food & Environment Reporting Network (FERN)*, April 22. Available at: <https://thefern.org/2020/04/mapping-covid-19-in-meat-and-food-processing-plants/> (Accessed: May 12, 2021).

Davis, T. J. 2020, 'Family Seeks Workers Compensation Payment from Tyson after Iowa and Dies of COVID-19', *Des Moines Register*, June 18. Available at: <https://www.desmoinesregister.com/story/news/crime-and-courts/2020/06/10/family-tyson-worker-who-died-covid-19-files-workers-comp-case/5337162002/> (Accessed May 12, 2021).

Kousch, A. 2020, 'Community Health and Women as Healers: Profiles in Resilience', *Women, Food and Agriculture Network*, April 28. Available at: <https://wfan.org/news/2020/4/26/profiles-in-resilience> (Accessed May 12, 2021).

Roy, A. 2020, 'The Pandemic is a Portal', *Financial Times*, April 3. Available at: <https://www.ft.com/content/10d8f5e8-74eb-11ea-95fe-fcd274e920ca> (Accessed May 12, 2021).

Valdivia, S. M. 2020, 'Workers Sue Smithfield Foods, Allege Conditions Put Them at Risk for COVID-19', *National Public Radio*, April 24. <https://www.npr.org/2020/04/24/844644200/workers-sue-smithfield-foods-allege-conditions-put-them-at-risk-for-covid-19> (Accessed May 12, 2021).

Western U.P. Food Systems Collaborative (WUPFSC) n.d. Available at: <https://www.wupfoodsystems.com/growing-from-the-heart> (Accessed December 1, 2021).

White, M. 2018, *Freedom Farmers: Agricultural Resilience and the Black Freedom Movement*, University of North Carolina Press.

Women, Food and Agriculture Network n.d. 'About', Available at: <https://wfan.org/about-wfan> (Accessed: May 12, 2021).

Women, Food and Agriculture Network (WFAN) 2020a, 'Creative Community Support', March 17. Available at: <https://wfan.org/news/2020/3/17/creative-community-support> (Accessed May 12, 2021).

Women, Food and Agriculture Network (WFAN) 2020b, 'WFAN Statement in Solidarity with Movements for Black Lives', June 5. Available at: <https://wfan.org/news/2020/6/5/wfan-statement-in-solidarity-with-movements-for-black-lives> (Accessed May 12, 2021).

9 COVID-19, migrant workers, and meatpacking in US agriculture: a critical feminist reflection

Emily Southard

The COVID-19 pandemic has revealed many fault lines in our global agriculture system. Despite a long history of critique by scholars and activists, one glaring example is the simultaneous dependence on migrant[1] workers in agriculture and the way they are treated as disposable. While agriculture-related migration is universal, as a US resident currently living in the agricultural (and my home) state of Iowa, I will focus mainly on the plight of migrant workers here, employed in meatpacking. Migrant workers are the "backbone" of our agriculture system, yet arguably the most vulnerable of all US workers – constrained by the legalization of their humanity, overworked and undervalued, and most notably in the time of COVID-19, treated as expendable.

Broad effects of COVID-19 on migrant workers in US agriculture

The pandemic has profoundly affected mobility. From March 2020 to March 2021, migration processes and migrant laborers have been severely affected. For many working in the US industrial agriculture system, the reality has been a compulsory "life as normal" as their work is deemed essential and their workplaces deemed critical infrastructure – despite COVID-19 ravaging their workplaces, communities, homes, and bodies. Even before COVID-19, the mobility of these workers was consistently restricted due to legal status, language, poverty, and rurality. Today their mobility is further restricted as international borders have closed, making travel to home communities difficult if not impossible. Moreover, mobility for undocumented migrants is riskier than ever, as unhygienic and densely packed ICE facilities have experienced COVID-19 outbreaks. The Vera Institute of Justice has attempted to track infections at US Immigration and Customs Enforcement (ICE) facilities reported by ICE themselves – as of March 2021, 9,686 cases and 21 deaths

DOI: 10.4324/9781003198277-12

have been reported. However, the Vera Institute's epidemiological model suggests ICE has underreported cases (Smart and Garcia, 2021). Thus, detention for migrants could mean loss of life, long-term health consequences, and trauma, not to mention the forestalling of migrant work's economic benefits.

While effects on mobility are universal, COVID-19's risk to workers in fields and factories depends on the nature of their work, legal status, geographic location, and local response. Workers who do field work may be able to socially distance, yet remain challenged while traveling to work or living in densely packed group quarters, a common migrant housing situation. Workers in industrialized or factory-style workplaces such as milking facilities, mushroom houses, and meatpacking plants face the most risk due to worker density. The infection rates of food sectors depending on their industry of employment has been carefully tracked by Douglas with the Food and Environment Reporting Network since April 2020. Undercounting is an issue even given Douglas's thorough data collection, as it still relies on reports from companies, local governments, and media. However, the data demonstrates how meatpacking workers have been disproportionately affected. As of March, 2021, 88,022 food sector workers have contracted COVID-19 with the vast majority – 57,526 workers – employed in meatpacking. Further, 375 food sector workers have died as a result of the virus, 284 of these deaths those of meatpacking workers (Douglas, 2021). Thus, I will now turn to my home state of Iowa, where meatpacking has exemplified the worst effects of COVID-19, due to the intersection of such work's risk and precarity, critical infrastructure status, and the structured vulnerability of workers.

Case study of meatpacking

Approximately 40 percent of meatpacking workers – 175,000 people – are migrants, and "meatpacking has the fifth-highest concentration of refugee workers" (Groves and Tareen, 2020). Migrant refugee workers are highly concentrated in Iowa's meatpacking industry which employs an average of 26,543 people (Stuesse and Dollar, 2020). Iowa has the second largest number of meatpacking workers in the country, following neighboring Nebraska. Pork plants dot the landscape where hogs outnumber people seven to one – JBS in Marshalltown and Ottumwa; Tyson in Waterloo, Columbus Junction, Independence, Storm Lake, Council Bluffs, and Perry; and Seaboard Triumph in Sioux City – just to name some of the major plants. Cattle and poultry are also processed here, at Iowa Premium Beef in Tama or Agri Star in Postville (formerly Agriprocessors, site of the infamous 2008 raid which led to the detainment and deportation of 398 and 297 Latinx workers, respectively).

The reliance on migrant workers in the meatpacking industry is an intentional product of how the sector is structured to maximize profit and minimize worker resistance. In the 1980s and 1990s, following consolidation of the industry, meatpacking plants sprung up across the rural Midwest. Work in these factories was mechanized and deskilled, meaning workers did not need to possess particular skills or experience, but rather, needed only to be willing to accept low wages for the dangerous and physically demanding work. "Cheap, easily replaceable labor, therefore, is key to the success of the industrial model in meatpacking" (Champlin and Hake, 2006, p. 55). Migrant workers made ideal candidates for this work for numerous reasons. Due to global inequities, their supply is virtually limitless and they accept wages far lower than US workers would for the same work. Further, migrant workers are unlikely to organize due to language and legal barriers. The fact that migrant workers are largely people of color living in a country founded on white supremacy contributes to a paradigm where workers are seen as machinery, not people, and "not as important as a bag of meat" (Ramos et al., 2021, p. 87).

The diversity of ethnicities, races, and languages of meatpacking workers in rural Iowa may seem like an achievement of multiculturalism. Yet, the reality is that workers (and their families) face a great deal of exploitation, isolation, and challenges in these transnational communities. Meatpacking jobs may pay well comparable to other available livelihoods. However, the average US$12.50 an hour wage means individuals and families supporting themselves – and potentially remitting to families back home – often live in relative poverty. Residential areas for migrants employed in meatpacking are thus typically visibly shoddier and less well-maintained than areas that house white residents. Natural disasters, including a tornado that hit Marshalltown in 2018 and a derecho that devastated Waterloo in August 2020, have particularly impacted migrant neighborhoods. These poorly constructed and maintained houses and apartment complexes, while affordable, were most vulnerable to the destruction wrought by the high winds of both weather events.

Rural Iowa's healthcare, education, and social service sectors are also not well-adapted to meeting the needs of these diverse and largely impoverished communities. For instance, as of 2019, nearly 20 percent of Ottumwa, Iowa's 4,655 students have limited English proficiency. Their ethnicities and languages are very heterogeneous, representing numerous ethnic groups from Mexico, El Salvador, Myanmar, Sudan, Ethiopia, and more. This diversity includes children of meatpacking workers from the Marshall Islands, whose language, Marshallese, is spoken only by approximately 50,000 people worldwide, making interpreters hard to find. NGOs attempt to fill the gaps between state resources and migrant needs, but their efforts have been further taxed by challenges presented by COVID-19. Plants employ interpreters, and information for employees – such as fliers JBS shared on Facebook in March 2021 about vaccination of workers in Marshalltown – are often provided in English, Spanish, Burmese, and French (for those from central and east Africa). Workers' language skills and legal status already pose issues for worker safety in a dangerous workplace environment where injuries are common (Ramos et al., 2021). Thus, given the pandemic, Joe Henry, vice-president of a national Latino activist group stated "immigrant or undocumented workers may be reluctant to complain about unsafe work conditions. And workers for whom English is not their first language may not fully understand the COVID-19 threat" (Eller, 2020a). Even pre-pandemic, these workers and their families faced numerous challenges, including poverty, poor housing, cultural isolation, inadequate access to state services, safety and work hazards, and legal concerns based on immigrant status. The exacerbation of their marginalization and exploitation is thus unsurprising in the context of the pandemic.

The risk imposed by the tight quarters and quick spread of COVID-19 in meatpacking plants has been compounded by the structured precarity of work in the industry which already positioned workers as dependent and replaceable. Workers, unable to endure lost income or potential reprisals for missing shifts, continue to clock in even when exhibiting symptoms of COVID-19. As documented by *The New York Times* "One worker [at a Tyson plant in Waterloo, Iowa] who died had taken Tylenol before entering the plant to lower her temperature enough to pass the screening, afraid that missing work would mean forgoing a bonus" (Swanson, Yaffe-Bellany, and Corkery, 2020). The plant's accountability in incentivizing workers with COVID-19 symptoms to continue to work is further substantiated by the fact that "[s]everal workers said the Tyson plant penalized people with 'points' for missing work if they or their families had COVID-19 symptoms" (Czyzon, 2021). Plants such as the Waterloo Tyson shut down for mere days to attempt to implement safety protocols, which were rudimentary at best and ineffective at worst. Workers reported that no major changes had been made and that the nature of the dense workplace required them to forego recommended distancing protocols (Czyzon, 2021). Thus, according to Douglas (2021), as of March 2021, 6,600 meatpacking workers in Iowa have fallen ill with COVID-19 across 26 plants, and 22 have died. These numbers are undoubtedly an undercount. The state of Iowa initially reported 444 cases at the Tyson plant in Waterloo, but county officials later updated that figure to 1031 positive cases out of 1,300 total employees (Foley, 2020; Swanson, Yaffe-Bellany, and Corkery, 2020). Moreover, testing and healthcare may be inaccessible due to language barriers or fears of detainment based on legal status, suggesting further undercounting on top of underreporting.

Undercounting and underreporting are made more insidious by the fact that managers and supervisors at the Waterloo Tyson plant clearly knew about the danger workers were facing and exacerbated that danger. Evidence has since revealed that higher-ups instructed interpreters to minimize the risk of COVID-19 and discourage the use of masks. Further, managers and supervisors made bets on infection rates of workers. This intentional deception and betting pool was brought to light by families of workers who died from the virus, who have since raised wrongful death lawsuits. While the lawsuits are ongoing as of March 2021, seven managers were fired from the Waterloo plant as a result of their participation in the betting. Seen in the context of how meatpacking has been structured to exploit those most vulnerable – migrant workers – this betting incident exemplifies the dehumanization of meatpacking workers. Due to their migrant status and the structuring of the industry to deskill and devalue work, migrant workers in meatpacking are treated as machinery, not people. This was echoed by Joe Henry, quoted in the *Des Moines Register*, who stated explicitly "[m]anagers don't see these people as humans ... [t]hey're just part of the machinery ... [w]orkers are viewed as expendable instead of essential" (Eller, 2020b).

Some government oversight was conducted in relation to COVID-19 spread in meatpacking plants, though the state, at best, failed to protect workers, and at worst, knowingly sacrificed workers' lives to maintain the agricultural economy. OSHA inspected only five of the major meatpacking plants in the state as of September 2020, determining only one plant had violated workplace safety regulations. The plant – Iowa Premium Beef Plant in Tama – was charged a mere US$957 for undercounting COVID-19 infections reported to the public (Associated Press, 2020). This minor fine for risking the lives of workers, their families, and their communities is particularly concerning when considering how the meatpacking industry has profited from the pandemic. For instance, meatpackers' middle-man status for beef served them to make record high profits in April and May 2020. As a result of panic over meat availability, consumer demand caused prices for beef products to surge. Simultaneously, live cattle prices fell precipitously due to concerns over processing facilities continuing to function given COVID-19 outbreaks. As meatpacking was deemed critical infrastructure by the federal government in late April, plants were forced to stay open and companies reaped the benefits while workers suffered. The "price spread," or profit that meatpackers received during this period averaged US$279 per hundred pounds of beef, an incredible increase compared to the average price spread from 2016 to 2018 – US$21 per hundred pounds of beef (Fu, 2020).

Gendered implications

Much of this situation is gendered. Most obvious is the recorded gender differences in mortality from COVID-19, wherein men are particularly at risk of death from the virus. This is notable as USDA data reports that 75 percent of hired farm laborers are men. While USDA data does not provide a gendered breakdown of migrant farm laborers specifically, it does report that 72 percent of these hired farmworkers are foreign-born. Moreover, studies have demonstrated that migration to the US for this kind of work is men-dominated, though with growing numbers of women. In meatpacking specifically, 64 percent of workers are men (Stuesse and Dollar, 2020). These men's gender, migrant, and class identities may also intersect in their willingness and ability to access healthcare services. Norms of masculinity may converge with concerns about language, legal status, and cost, deterring migrant men from seeking healthcare even if ill with COVID-19.

The paradigm of lone man migrant worker has emotional and psychological effects for both migrant, alone and at-risk in a foreign community, and for his family back home. Men migrant workers living in the US alone must face the isolation, fear, and inability to travel, without direct familial support, and often in communities which exclude them due to their race, ethnicity, language, and/or legal status. Numerous studies have also demonstrated that women "left behind" by spousal migration face great emotional strain, even without the compounding effect of a pandemic. As "left-behind" wives have expressed in normal circumstances that their husband's absence causes them feelings of isolation, loneliness, difficulty in managing financial responsibilities, and difficulty in making decisions in emergency situations, it is doubtless that the increased fear of illness, isolation of lockdowns, and financial strains caused by the pandemic worsen these issues.

Unique gendered implications for women migrant agricultural workers can also be assumed, as previous research has demonstrated emotional stress for mothers who migrate and are unable to fulfill caretaking duties in their home countries, an emotional toll that is exacerbated during the pandemic. Mothers working abroad must not only worry about their own safety while continuing to work and facing exposure to the virus, but also must manage concerns about their children and kin's safety and financial stability. An additional consideration for settled families is school closures, and the increased caretaking duties for women especially, a topic covered by others in this anthology. A personal source working with these communities described how the pandemic has caused a shortage of childcare options, forcing many mothers to choose between losing their livelihoods or leaving children at home unattended. Lastly, constrained economic situations and the stress of the pandemic could worsen household tensions and gender-based violence, as seen in previous crises and natural disasters. These concerns about the pandemic's effects on women's increased care work burden, heightened household tensions, and higher rates of domestic violence are again exacerbated by migrant workers' identities. Language and legal status pose serious intersectional challenges on what type of help and resources women may be able to access.

Conclusion

This chapter only begins to cover some of the numerous intersectional and gendered effects that COVID-19 is having on migrants in agriculture. But this geographically constrained snapshot surfaces some of the depth and breadth of exploitation related to migration in agriculture essential to the modern agrifood system. Exploitation and disregard for migrants' lives are certainly not limited to the farms, fields, and meatpacking plants of the United States, but rather has become part and parcel of the race-to-the-bottom of neoliberal capitalism. The transnational interconnectedness of migrant worker precarity and vulnerability is evidenced by the disproportionate effect the pandemic has had on migrant workers in the United States and beyond. The intersection of migrant workers' racialized, illegalized, and gendered identities in the United States and globally has been structured – as demonstrated by the meatpacking industry – to permit workers as little power as possible, leaving them in a highly precarious position, materially and mentally, even in the best of circumstances. COVID-19 has just provided an unfortunate opportunity for the barbaric effects of the globalized division of labor in agriculture to be particularly revealed and for the way that gender interacts in these circumstances to be specifically analyzed.

Note

1 I use "migrant worker" throughout this piece to include temporary migrant workers, immigrants, and refugees, regardless of legal status.

References

Associated Press (2020) 'After inspecting 5 meatpacking plants with COVID-19 outbreaks, Iowa regulators only fine $957', *The Gazette*. Available at: https://www.thegazette.com/subject/news/business/after-inspecting-5-meatpacking-plants-where-thousands-of-workers-were-sickened-iowa-regulators-issue-one-fine-957-20200924.

Champlin, D. and Hake, E. (2006) 'Immigration as industrial strategy in American meatpacking', *Review of Political Economy*, 18(1), pp. 49–70. doi: 10.1080/09538250500354140.

Czyzon, S. (2021) 'Criminal records leave Tyson workers feeling stuck at Waterloo plant', *The Courier*. Available at: https://wcfcourier.com/news/criminal-records-leave-tyson-workers-feeling-stuck-at-waterloo-plant/article_a4f1577e-5f0d-51fd-8fb3-0db521e052b8.html.

Douglas, L. (2021) *Mapping Covid-19 Outbreaks in the Food System*, Food and Environment Reporting Network. Available at: https://thefern.org/2020/04/mapping-covid-19-in-meat-and-food-processing-plants/.

Eller, D. (2020a) 'Iowa JBS workers tell advocates they're packed in too tight to stay safe from coronavirus', *The Des Moines Register*, 31 March. Available at: https://www.desmoinesregister.com/story/money/agriculture/2020/03/31/iowa-meatpacking-workers-space-insufficient-protect-jbs-plant-coronavirus/5087544002/.

Eller, D. (2020b) "Tyson fires 7 managers at Waterloo pork plant tied to alleged betting on how many workers COVID-19 would sicken," *The Des Moines Register*, 16 December. Available at: https://www.desmoinesregister.com/story/money/agriculture/2020/12/16/tyson-foods-fires-seven-waterloo-iowa-plant-managers-betting-covid-19/3927478001/.

Foley, R. J. (2020) 'Outbreak at Iowa pork plant was larger than state reported', *The Washington Post*, 22 July. Available at: https://www.washingtonpost.com/business/outbreak-at-iowa-pork-plant-was-larger-than-state-reported/2020/07/22/5a47c9fe-cc32-11ea-99b0-8426e26d203b_story.html.

Fu, J. (2020) 'Beef packers' profit margins reach historic levels during the height of Covid-19 plant shutdowns', *The Counter*, 24 July. Available at: https://thecounter.org/beef-packers-profit-margins-reached-historic-levels-covid-19-plant-shutdowns/.

Groves, S. and Tareen, S. (2020) 'U.S. meatpacking industry relies on immigrant workers. But a labor shortage looms', *Los Angeles Times*, 26 May. Available at: https://www.latimes.com/food/story/2020-05-26/meatpacking-industry-immigrant-undocumented-workers.

Ramos, A. K. *et al.* (2021) '"No somos máquinas" (We are not machines): Worker perspectives of safety culture in meatpacking plants in the Midwest', *American Journal of Industrial Medicine*, 64(2), pp. 84–96. doi: 10.1002/ajim.23206.

Smart, N. and Garcia, A. (2021) *Tracking COVID-19 in Immigration Detention*, Vera Institute of Justice. Available at: https://www.vera.org/tracking-covid-19-in-immigration-detention.

Stuesse, A. and Dollar, N. T. (2020) *Who are America's Meat and Poultry Workers?*, Economic Policy Institute. Available at: https://www.epi.org/blog/meat-and-poultry-worker-demographics/.

Swanson, A., Yaffe-Bellany, D. and Corkery, M. (2020) 'Pork Chops vs. People: Battling Coronavirus in an Iowa Meat Plant', *The New York Times*, 10 May. Available at: https://www.nytimes.com/2020/05/10/business/economy/coronavirus-tyson-plant-iowa.html.

10 Queerness in the US agrifood system during COVID-19

Michaela Hoffelmeyer

Introduction

Although research and data frequently erase queer people in agriculture, queer people engage in all aspects of the agrifood system, from the farm – as farmworkers and farmers – to the table – as restaurant workers, owners, and consumers. As such, there is no singular queer agricultural pandemic experience. This chapter outlines the multifaceted ways that COVID-19 impacts queer people at various points in the United States' agrifood system. I emphasize that queer food workers and farmworkers' experiences are influenced by intersections of race, ethnicity, class, and gender as queerness traverses these identities. I highlight how continued disparities in healthcare, economics, and social support call for policies that attend to this heterogeneous group, especially in times of crisis.

Food and farmworkers

For essential workers in the agrifood system, the pandemic poses a double-edged sword. Employment provides income and potentially access to health insurance, but working in fields, processing plants, and restaurants with limited personal protective equipment and inadequate worker safety protocols poses health risks. At the same time, losing jobs or withdrawing from unsafe work conditions may allow these people to avoid COVID-19 at the expense of losing vital income. Agrifood system workers face a higher risk of being exposed to COVID-19 due to the essential nature of their work. For queer people in these jobs, if exposed, there is a significant risk of becoming seriously ill as queer populations face higher rates of poverty and less access to medical care than their heterosexual peers (Whittington, Hadfield, and Calderón, 2020) (Figure 10.1).

DOI: 10.4324/9781003198277-13

Figure 10.1 Queer farmer, Alysha Gareis, tends the livestock on California farm. During 2020, intense wildfires and COVID-19 forced significant shifts in farmers' market safety protocols and threatened Alysha's employment options (Alysha Gareis).

Farmworkers

Farmworkers are the foundation of the food system and have been deemed "essential" during COVID-19 despite frequently experiencing racism and xenophobia (Holmes, 2013). Of the 2.4 million farmworkers in the United States (Farmworker Justice, 2018) there is no count of the number of queer farmworkers, but they are in the fields and sharing their stories (Lizarazo et al., 2017). In addition to healthcare barriers faced by all farmworkers (e.g., cost, access, fear of employer retaliation), queer farmworkers face stigma and fear for revealing their identity in healthcare settings, potentially placing them at higher risk for adverse health outcomes (National LGBT Health Education Center and Farmworker Justice, 2015). For farmworkers during the pandemic, the combined heteronormativity and heterosexism in agriculture and healthcare may result in underdiagnosing and insufficient tracing of COVID-19 (Wypler and Hoffelmeyer, 2020). The National LGBT Health Education Center's policy brief lays out best practices for health centers to build trust with queer farmworkers, such as inclusive language and availability of sexual health screenings (National LGBT Health Education Center and Farmworker Justice, 2015). As farmworkers are required to continue working during this time of increased health risks, healthcare facilities must adopt these best practices to support queer farmworkers' well-being.

Meat processing workers

In ethnographic fieldwork in the rural South, Ribas (2016) notes a surprising number of queer employees, particularly African Americans, involved in meat processing. COVID-19 has been particularly devastating for meat processing workers (Douglas, 2020). Meat processing facilities remain hotbeds for COVID-19 due to poor working conditions that require close and prolonged contact among workers and slow implementation of safety protocols from companies. Inadequate medical care, lack of paid time off, and low wages in this industry are exacerbated by heterosexism. Compared to heterosexual populations, queer populations report avoiding seeking medical attention because of costs and discrimination (Whittington, Hadfield, and Calderón, 2020). When considered alongside existing research documenting meat processing workers' injury rates (Horowitz, 2008), queer people in this industry may face additional hurdles to remaining safe and healthy during the pandemic.

Restaurant workers

Restaurant and food services represent the highest employment industry of queer people (Whittington, Hadfield, and Calderón, 2020). Approximately 2 million queer people work in this industry, representing 15 percent of the queer population (Whittington, Hadfield and Calderón, 2020). During the pandemic, restaurant and food service workers lost their jobs or experienced severely reduced hours, thereby increasing economic insecurity for this population. Because healthcare in the United States is tied to work, the loss of employment is further devastating during the pandemic. Because queer people work in service industries at higher rates than their heterosexual peers (Whittington, Hadfield, and Calderón, 2020), the pandemic's impact on the restaurant and food service industry has likely unevenly impacted queer populations.

Food and farmworker considerations

Federal financial and health support misses populations, in particular undocumented immigrants who are heavily involved in food production (Holmes, 2013), processing (Ribas, 2016), and service (Jayaraman, 2013). Being queer and undocumented can compound existing healthcare inequalities. For example, immigrant workers, in particular undocumented workers, in farming, meat processing, and food services remain at work even when sick, due to low pay, lack of paid sick time, and fear of employer retaliation (Holmes, 2013; Jayaraman, 2013; Ribas, 2016). Additionally, queer workers report fears of discrimination that prevent them from requesting leave if required to disclose their identity (Whittington, Hadfield, and Calderón, 2020). During COVID-19, queer workers, particularly those in precarious employment, may be hesitant to report exposure to or contraction of COVID-19 due to any combination of social location factors. Considering sexuality and gender identity along with health risks associated with immigration status, race, and ethnicity, offers the potential to understand the experiences of these populations more fully. Given the multiplying effects of COVID-19, this pandemic demonstrates the power of centering the health and well-being of the most vulnerable in the agrifood system as a necessary means of facilitating safe and reliable production, processing, and distribution of food (Wypler and Hoffelmeyer, 2020) (Figure 10.2).

Figure 10.2 Farm sunrise on a queer-owned farm in Pennsylvania, captured during morning chores (Michaela Hoffelmeyer).

Farm owners

The queer community is no stranger to being physically distant and isolated from social support as our fellow queers and chosen family are often geographically dispersed. For queer farmers, in-person queer-centered events offer a chance to relieve social and physical isolation and develop economic networking opportunities (Wypler, 2019). Queer community gatherings offer a place of vital respite and networking, especially for queer people navigating heterosexism in agriculture (Hoffelmeyer, 2020). However, many of these in-person meetings were canceled due to the pandemic. The loss of social support, knowledge transfer, and networking due to COVID-19 is immeasurable.

Queer farmers during COVID-19 face increased mental health stressors related to the loss of in-person social networking and support (Wypler and Hoffelmeyer, 2020), as both the queer (Salerno, Williams and Gattamorta, 2020) and farmer (Inwood et al., 2019) populations face higher mental health risks compared to the general population in non-pandemic times. However, because queer farmers have formed resilience social support networks in the face of anticipated heterosexism, queer farmers may have insulated themselves against some adverse mental health impacts during the pandemic (Wypler and Hoffelmeyer, 2020). As such, while mental health and support networks are critical for all farmers, queer farmers offer new insights about the role of building collective, wide-ranging community support systems that can weather existing inequalities and offer protection under increased stress during the pandemic and potentially other extreme events such as climate change.

Farm policy

Queer farmers, often small-scale and sustainable, have unique policy needs that cannot be assumed to be addressed through sweeping legislation. During COVID-19, small-scale farms with already tight profit margins are rapidly adjusting to online sales, increased safety measures, and lost wholesale and event revenue. Despite experiencing financial hardship, small-scale farms rarely receive adequate financial support compared to large-scale commodity farms. Federal farm subsidy programs direct aid toward the wealthiest farms (Schechinger, 2021). Under the Trump administration, the Coronavirus Financial Assistance Program aimed to support agricultural producers but likely missed small farmers due to challenges accounting for losses of direct sales and costs associated with diversified production (Crampton, 2020). While data is still emerging, through June of 2020, nearly 24 percent of farm subsidies went to the top 1 percent of farms, and approximately 64 percent of subsidies went to the top 10 percent (Schechinger, 2021). Rather than continuing the status quo of disproportionately supporting large-scale commodity producers, funds directed toward small-scale producers are critical for agrifood system resilience, particularly in times of crisis.

Farm scale and identity are tightly interconnected. Government aid funneled toward large-scale producers means that men – often white and likely heterosexual – reap the benefits of US farm subsidies (Sachs et al., 2016), predominantly because crop subsidies favor wheat, corn, grain, and other staple crops (Howard, 2016), and men tend to be engaged in highly mechanized, capital-intensive production (Sachs et al., 2016). As such, COVID-19 farm aid should center socially disadvantaged farmers. The US Department of Agriculture (USDA) has a history of discrimination against minorities, including Blacks, Hispanics, and women (Carpenter, 2012). In the wake of COVID-19, small farms may benefit from increased customer interest in sourcing food directly from farmers. However, these farmers may ultimately be excluded from government support if programs are not specifically geared to underserved farming populations. Unlike race, ethnicity, and (cis)gender, the USDA does not consider queer (not heterosexual and/or cis-gender) farmers to be an underserved population. Qualitative research demonstrates that queer farmers face barriers in accessing government farming assistance (Leslie, 2017). Therefore, in addition to COVID-19 farm aid being directed to underserved farming groups, USDA programs should expand to include support for queer farmers as heterosexism has been documented in agriculture. While the Biden administration shows promise for supporting the distribution of financial resources to Black farmers (Walljasper, 2021), long-term structural changes confronting concentration in land, decision-making, and power in agriculture will be required to deter the high levels of inequitable distribution of resources and injustices currently existing in agriculture (Hendrickson et al., 2020) (Figure 10.3).

Consumers

Queer consumers experience disproportionate levels of food insecurity and Supplemental Nutrition Assistance Program (SNAP) participation outside of global pandemics (Brown, Romero and Gates, 2016). In 2016, approximately 17 percent of heterosexual adults experienced a time when they did not have enough money to feed themselves or their families; that number was 27% – or 2.2 million people – for queer adults (Brown, Romero and Gates, 2016). Within the queer community, food access is unevenly distributed by race and ethnicity as 42 percent of African Americans, 33 percent of Hispanics, 32 percent of American Indians and Alaskan Natives, and 21 percent of Whites reported not having enough money to feed themselves or their families (Brown, Romero and Gates, 2016). Efforts to expand SNAP and provide emergency food access must confront the existing inequalities in food access.

Conclusion

This chapter demonstrates queer people's involvement in every facet of the agrifood system from farm to table. While heterosexism and heteronormativity make this population seemingly invisible, considering the unique needs of queer populations remains vital for addressing inequalities and injustices in the agrifood system. Recognizing the critical role of gender and sexuality,

Figure 10.3 Naomi's Organic Farm Supply, Portland, Oregon, operated for over 11 years but closed in 2021 after dramatic shifts in safety protocols and sales operations due to the pandemic (Michaela Hoffelmeyer).

queer people in the agrifood system have mobilized during COVID-19. For example, Rock Steady Farm, a revolutionary, highly visible queer-owned farm in rural New York, worked before and throughout the pandemic to meet the needs of queer and BIPOC (Black, indigenous, people of color) customers and farmers. Rock Steady makes nutrient-dense food available to BIPOC, queer, and low-income communities through the farm's innovative sliding-scale Community Supported Agriculture model and Food Sovereignty Fund. In 2020 at the height of the pandemic, 57 percent of food grown at Rock Steady went to low-income consumers, representing approximately 52,000 meals and 35,000 pounds of produce (Rock Steady Farm & Flowers, n.d.). Additionally, Rock Steady's farmer training and land access partnerships promote long-term, sustainable shifts in the agrifood system (Rock Steady Farm & Flowers, no date). By creating a safe, supportive farm where BIPOC and queer farm employees can learn valuable farming skills, Rock Steady's model counters racism and heterosexism in farming, which can deter farmers' long-term involvement in agriculture (Hoffelmeyer, 2021). Working against exploitative models by privileging farm employees' livable wages and making significant efforts during COVID-19 to protect farmers' safety, Rock Steady illustrates one farming model that confronts rather than replicates injustices.

Other efforts to support queer community health include the Out in the Open organization, the Okra Project, and the Queer Food Foundation. First, the rural queer grassroots organization, Out in the Open, located in Vermont, developed online programing and support groups to relieve isolation and promote organizing around rural trans and queer health. Out in the Open hosted a virtual meeting for queer farmers to gather and network about the impacts of COVID-19 (Out in the Open, n.d.). Second, The Okra Project works in New Jersey, Philadelphia, and New York to address food and economic inequalities faced by Black Trans people. Early in the pandemic, the organization expanded its international grocery fund in anticipation of increased need. Adjusting to COVID-19 and Center for Disease Control guidelines, the organization plans to revive its Direct Chef Services program during 2021, which hires Black Trans chefs to prepare nutritious and culturally specific meals delivered directly to Black Trans people (The Okra Project, n.d.). Finally, the Queer Food Foundation aims to "promote, protect, fund, and create queer food spaces; to acknowledge, celebrate, and honor queer food workers and chefs." Founded in 2020, the Queer Food Foundation has begun creating a queer food database and developed the Queer Food Fund, a community mutual aid project redistributing donations to the Black Queer community facing food insecurity (Queer Food Foundation, no date).

These are simply a few examples of queer people resisting oppression and marginalization embedded in the agrifood system. As non-profit organizations, these examples illustrate how federal and state-level support is insufficient. Pivoting to meet community members' needs during the pandemic, these organizations are filling critical roles. However, long-term changes to the agrifood system requires attention to the distribution of access to land, labor, and knowledge at all levels of agricultural production with attention to racism, classism, sexism, and heterosexism (Leslie, 2019).

COVID-19 exposed the numerous cracks in the standardized global food system (Hendrickson, 2020), yet the shortcomings of the current agrifood system were already visible to those experiencing food injustices. While COVID-19 data is still emerging, trends show that Black, Indigenous, Hispanic (Wood, 2020), and queer communities (National LGBT Cancer Network, 2020) are disproportionately affected. Moving forward, policies that center these communities' insights and perspectives on food production and access will be critical to bolstering resilience and sustainability in the agrifood system.

References

Farmworker Justice (2018) *Selected Statistics on Farmworkers*. Available at: https://www.farmworkerjustice.org/sites/default/files/resources/NAWSdatafactsht10-18-18.pdf.

Brown, T. N. T., Romero, A. P. and Gates, G. J. (2016) *Food Insecurity and SNAP Participation in the LGBT Community*, The Williams Institute, UCLA School of Law. Available at: http://williamsinstitute.law.ucla.edu/wp-content/uploads/Food-Insecurity-and-SNAP-Participation-in-the-LGBT-Community.pdf.

Carpenter, S. (2012) 'The USDA Discrimination Cases: Pigford, In Re Black Farmers, Keepseagle, Garcia, and Love', *Drake Journal of Agricultural Law*, 17(1), pp. 1–36.

Crampton, L. (2020) Young Farmers Worry About Access to USDA Aid, *Politico*. Available at: https://www.politico.com/newsletters/morning-agriculture/2020/05/29/young-farmers-worry-about-access-to-usda-aid-788003.

Douglas, L. (2020) *Mapping Covid-19 in Meat and Food Processing Plants*, Food and Environment Reporting Network. Available at: https://thefern.org/2020/04/mapping-covid-19-in-meat-and-food-processing-plants/.

Hendrickson, M. K. (2020) 'Covid Lays Bare the Brittleness of a Concentrated and Consolidated Food System', *Agriculture and Human Values*, 37, pp. 579–580. https://link.springer.com/article/10.1007%2Fs10460-020-10092-y#citeas.

Hendrickson, M. K. *et al.* (2020) *The Food System: Concentration and Its Impacts*, Family Farm Action Alliance. Available at: https://farmactionalliance.org/concentrationreport/.

Hoffelmeyer, M. (2020) 'Queer Farmers: Sexuality on the Farm', in Sachs, C. et al. (eds) *Gender and Agriculture Handbook*. New York: Routledge, pp. 348–359.

Hoffelmeyer, M. (2021) '"Out" on the Farm: Queer Farmers Maneuvering Heterosexism and Visibility', *Rural Sociology*. Available at: https://onlinelibrary. wiley.com/doi/full/10.1111/ruso.12378?casa_token=F67_U7vGT3wAAAAA% 3A9FBXtiISNG64Dv3QlIbaJRV7t73B_pGLQYW4ZvcnBcNTNvua7X-2QI_ Rsavs0_SW9cvJAyQQ-YOTEWQ.

Holmes, S. (2013) *Fresh Fruit, Broken Bodies: Migrant Farmworkers in the United States*. Berkeley, CA: University of California Press.

Horowitz, R. (2008) '"That Was a Dirty Job!" Technology and Workplace Hazards in Meatpacking over the Long Twentieth Century', *Labor: Studies in Working-Class History of the Americas*, 5(2), pp. 13–25. doi: 10.1215/15476715-2007-075.

Howard, P. (2016) *Concentration and Power in the Food System: Who Controls What We Eat?* New York: Bloomsbury.

Inwood, S. *et al.* (2019) 'Responding to Crisis: Farmer Mental Health Programs in the Extension North Central Region', *Journal of Extension*, 57(6). Available at: https://openprairie.sdstate.edu/cgi/viewcontent.cgi?article=1078&context= chd_pubs.

Jayaraman, S. (2013) *Behind the Kitchen Door*. Ithaca: Cornell University Press.

Leslie, I. S. (2017) 'Queer Farmers: Sexuality and the Transition to Sustainable Agriculture', *Rural Sociology*, 82(4), pp. 747–771. doi: 10.1111/ruso.12153.

Leslie, I. S. (2019) 'Queer Farmland: Land Access Strategies for Small-Scale Agriculture', *Society and Natural Resources*. Routledge, 32(8), pp. 928–946. doi :10.1080/08941920.2018.1561964.

Lizarazo, T. *et al.* (2017) 'Ethics, Collaboration, and Knowledge Production: Digital Storytelling with Sexually Diverse Farmworkers in California', *Lateral*, 6(1). Available at: https://mdsoar.org/handle/11603/19531.

National LGBT Cancer Network (2020) *Coronavirus Information*. Available at: https://cancer-network.org/coronavirus-2019-lgbtq-info/.

National LGBT Health Education Center and Farmworker Justice (2015) *Promoting Health Care Access to Lesbian, Gay, Bisexual, and Transgender (LGBT) Farmworkers*. Available at: https://www.farmworkerjustice.org/sites/default/ files/FJ-LGBTHealthEducationCenterIssueBrief FINAL.pdf.

Out in the Open (no date). Available at: https://www.weareoutintheopen.org/.

Queer Food Foundation (no date). Available at: https://queerfoodfoundation.org/.

Ribas, V. (2016) *On the line: Slaughterhouse Lives and the Making of the New South*. Oakland, CA: University of California Press.

Rock Steady Farm & Flowers (no date). Available at: https://www.rocksteadyfarm .com/.

Sachs, C. *et al.* (2016) *The Rise of Women Farmers and Sustainable Agriculture*. Iowa City: University of Iowa Press.

Salerno, J. P., Williams, N. D. and Gattamorta, K. A. (2020) "LGBTQ Populations: Psychologically Vulnerable Communities in the COVID-19 Pandemic," *Psychological Trauma: Theory, Research, Practice, and Policy*, 12, pp. 239– 242. doi: 10.1037/tra0000837.

Schechinger, A. (2021) *Under Trump, Farm Subsidies Soared and the Rich Got Richer Biden and Congress Must Reform a Wasteful and Unfair System*. Available at: https://www.ewg.org/interactive-maps/2021-farm-subsidies-ballooned-under -trump/.

The Okra Project (no date). Available at: https://www.theokraproject.com/.

Walljasper, C. (2021) "U.S. Lawmakers Introduce Legislation to Help Black Farmers," *Reuters*. Available at: https://www.reuters.com/article/us-usa -agriculture-relief/u-s-lawmakers-introduce-legislation-to-help-black-farmers -idUSKBN2A9333.

Whittington, C., Hadfield, K. and Calderón, C. (2020) *The Lives and Livelihoods of Many in the LGBTQ+ Community Are at Risk Amidst COVID-19 Crisis*, Human Rights Campaign. Available at: https://assets2.hrc.org/files/assets/resources /COVID19-IssueBrief-032020-FINAL.pdf?_ga=2.235306753.1276285206 .1615311115-319094525.1614199648

Wood, D. (2020) *As Pandemic Deaths Add Up, Racial Disparities Persist – And In Some Cases Worsen*, NPR. Available at: https://www.npr.org/sections/health -shots/2020/09/23/914427907/as-pandemic-deaths-add-up-racial-disparities -persist-and-in-some-cases-worsen?t=16085096925531&t=1612998003537.

Wypler, J. (2019) "Lesbian and Queer Sustainable Farmer Networks in the Midwest," *Society & Natural Resources*, 32(8), pp. 947–964. doi: 10.1080/08941920.2019.1584834.

Wypler, J. and Hoffelmeyer, M. (2020) "LGBTQ+ Farmer Health in COVID-19," *Journal of Agromedicine*, 25(4), pp. 370–373. doi: 10.1080/1059924X.2020. 1814923.

11 Food corporation allegiance or worker solidarity? Summoning restaurant worker solidarity in the age of COVID-19

Whitney Shervey

The death of Breonna Taylor and George Floyd in 2020 ignited the Black Lives Matter uprising that catalyzed the United States and beyond to face the death and destruction that is structural racism. Through this death and destruction comes life and restoration, unifying people to come together and fight against the systems that create and maintain systemic oppression. This rings true for the people of color who are challenging the inequities they face during the COVID-19 global pandemic. It has been over a year since the first case of COVID-19 was detected in the United States, causing a wave of constant change for everyone. As a global pandemic, COVID-19 is still wreaking havoc across the world and the food system. Food workers are a lynchpin to our survival, yet their essential function is often dismissed or forgotten. The intersection of COVID-19 and structural racism pandemics have unearthed injustices that have plagued restaurant workers for far too long, bringing to the surface the reality that our food system was built and thrives on structural racism.

At the intersection of gender and race, women of color are disproportionately impacted by low wages and face additional inequities brought on by the COVID-19 pandemic. Intersectionality recognizes that identities are complex, therefore how people benefit from or are disadvantaged by the power dynamics of social structures are distinctly variable. Many women of color work in low-paying fast-food jobs; a sector of the food industry that has been fairly resilient to the fluctuation of COVID-19 restrictions due to the convenience nature of the fast-food business model. Likewise, restaurants are searching for resilient measures to abide by COVID-19 protocols that in the end put workers at risk. This resiliency is reflected in corporate profits, not in the health and safety of the workers, leaving women of color who work in the restaurant industry no choice but to risk their lives to feed their own families. The restaurant industry's lack of paid sick leave and

DOI: 10.4324/9781003198277-14

health insurance forces women of color to work in unsafe environments with little choice to elevate their concerns. Accordingly, women of color are leading worker-led movements to challenge this risk and the many injustices restaurant workers endure. Restaurant corporations are quick to make statements claiming their commitment to addressing racism, yet their lack of cooperation with worker-led movements suggests their investments are elsewhere.

This chapter first examines structural racism in the restaurant industry and COVID-19. It then covers income inequality at the intersection of gender and race followed by the corporate response to the intersecting pandemics. Finally, it explores restaurant-worker-led movements in the face of COVID-19 and the Black Lives Matter uprising, ending with a summoning of solidarity.

Structural racism and COVID-19 within the food system are plaguing workers of color in an industry that is already known for having low standards for taking care of its employees. According to ongoing data on COVID-19 cases, hospitalizations, and deaths by race/ethnicity by the Centers for Disease Control and Prevention (2021), Black, African American, and non-Hispanic persons are reporting cases, hospitalizations, and deaths of COVID-19 at rates greater than those of white persons (CDC 2021). Additionally, social determinants of health play a role in comorbidities that put restaurant workers of color at greater risk of dying from COVID-19 once contracted (Nittle 2020). In other words, living in food apartheids, facing chronic food insecurity, and working in low-wage jobs like food service can create health conditions that increase complications or morbidity rates for people that contract COVID-19. Restaurant workers facing food insecurity that subsequently increases their risk of dying from COVID-19 is structural racism and a major flaw and injustice of the food system.

The restaurant industry has been hit hard by COVID-19 and the people impacted the most severely are the workers. Across the United States, restaurants have been forced to close their doors, lay off workers, and pivot their operations to abide by rules and regulations to limit the spread of COVID-19. Workers risk their lives to go to work, forcing them to place their lives in the hands of customers. Along with having their safety and well-being put into the hands of the customer, restaurant workers are in constant fear of unemployment due to the oscillating reopening phases that are determined by the state. Indeed, states deciding to tighten restrictions is a needed measure to mitigate the spread of COVID-19, yet the constant flux of employment–unemployment harms restaurant workers as they often do not know if their most recent paycheck will be their last.

The employment–unemployment flux is not the only threat to restaurant workers; in fact, the risk that restaurant workers are taking to feed America is a deadly one. A recent study evaluating the death records from the California Department of Public Health by sector/occupation and by race/ethnicity (Chen et al. 2021: 2–8) suggests that food and agriculture workers have the highest mortality rate from COVID-19 with excess mortality occurring in high-risk occupations, with the highest being cook, and also occurring for Black, Latino, and Asian workers across all sectors and occupations (Chen et al. 2021). To put it bluntly, restaurant workers are dying from COVID-19 at rates higher than other occupations and, regardless of occupation, Black, Latino, and Asian workers have a higher excess mortality rate. These higher mortality rates are likely because Black, Latino, and Asian workers make up the majority of the workforce in sectors and occupations deemed essential. It is concerning that food and agriculture workers have the highest mortality rate by occupation compared to healthcare workers, many of whom are taking care of COVID-19 patients. It is easy to understand why workers who are not essential and have the option to work from home are not represented in excess mortality rates from COVID-19. However, it is concerning that health care workers, who are often interacting directly with COVID-19 patients are not at as high a risk of contracting COVID-19 as are restaurant workers. Restaurant workers risking their lives to feed America with little to no option for protecting themselves from the risk of COVID-19 leads me to wonder why restaurant workers are at such high risk and why it is that they are unable to be protected from this risk.

Restaurant workers lack access to paid sick leave and health benefits, forcing them to contend with the paradox of protecting their own health, the health of others, and a paycheck with little to no support from employers or the food industry at large. According to the Food Chain Workers Alliance 2011 survey, of the 630 respondents, 60 percent of food system workers lack access to paid sick time and 58 percent do not have health care coverage (Lo and Oliva 2020: 103). In fact, the inadequate COVID-19 safety protocols and the lack of contact tracing within restaurant establishments puts restaurant workers at greater risk while on the job (Waxman 2020). Additionally, as states roll out their vaccine plans it is up to them to determine who they will prioritize. Some states have prioritized vaccinating restaurant workers in early phases while other states like Oregon have not (Frane 2021). This is troubling considering that many states are open or are reopening for indoor dining, therefore increasing the risk of restaurant workers contracting COVID-19 while on the job. Although I should know better by now, I am still shocked that the people we entrust with feeding the public are forced to choose between a paycheck and their own health. Before COVID-19, this was a public health issue that resulted in outbreaks of norovirus and other foodborne illnesses. In the age of COVID-19, the lack of access to sick leave and health benefits is compounding a public health crisis and is costing restaurant workers their lives. Ultimately, trust in leadership is dismal for restaurant workers especially for those workers bound by the low wage for tipped workers of US$2.13 an hour.

Restaurant workers making US$2.13 an hour are confronted with additional obstacles during COVID-19. In many states, tipped workers receive a minimum wage of US$2.13 from their employer assuming that with the tips that they receive they will bring home the state's non-tipped minimum wage. This form of wage structure is often referred to as a two-tier system and is highly problematic. Having a subminimum wage creates opportunities for employers to take advantage of tipped workers and leaves tipped workers vulnerable during times with little to no customer interface. On account of restrictions on indoor dining, many tipped workers have had their hours cut, been shifted to other duties, or been laid off. Additionally, workers that receive US$2.13 can find it difficult to receive unemployment because their wages are often seen as too low to qualify. Moreover, in the age of COVID-19, the delivery service landscape of how food is getting to customers is threatening wages for tipped workers by positioning tipped delivery drivers and tipped restaurant workers in a face-off over tips. Depending on the delivery service, who receives the tip varies among delivery service, restaurant, delivery driver, and restaurant worker. The reality is, delivery service corporations are benefiting the most from the increase in deliveries during COVID-19 (Sharma 2021). While some delivery services allow customers to tip the restaurant or delivery workers, others keep the tips for themselves, ultimately hurting restaurant workers at the intersection of gender and race.

Restaurant workers are distressed by low wages that are magnified by income inequality stratification along the lines of gender and race. Entmacher et al. (2014) report that women of color are disproportionately represented in low-wage work like fast-food and according to Reyes et al. (2015) are often segregated into the lowest-paying positions (Entmacher et al. 2014: 1; Reyes et al. 2015: 1). Segregated into the lowest-paid positions means that women often work for tips and in states with a tipped minimum wage of US$2.13 an hour, women are facing significant economic hardship during the global pandemic. Women work in food service occupations that are the lowest-paying and similar to income inequality across all sectors make less than their male counterparts working in the same occupation. On top of facing the lowest wages, women endure a culture of hypermasculinity and misogyny that normalizes sexual harassment and transphobia in the workplace. Both structural racism and gender inequality are at play here, making me wonder how corporations are responding.

The Black Lives Matter uprising that swept across the country and around the world in 2020 is not only a call to defund the police, but is also a call to address the structural racism that has forever plagued the United States. Following the days after George Floyd's death, fast-food corporations like McDonald's, Burger King, Wendy's, and the Pacific Northwest Burgerville fast-food chain made statements on how they are committed to addressing racism. Workers have challenged these corporations to address intersectional inequalities in their workplace and the corporations have fought back to silence workers and their demands. Knowing their anti-worker history, fast-food corporations announcing their support for the uprising is alarming. If fast-food corporations do not support those who are leading movements within their own companies to address the inequities they are experiencing, how can we trust that their commitments to addressing inequity will be met? Who will hold them accountable? (Figure 11.1)

Fast-food workers know their struggle and have been fighting to challenge fast-food corporations through worker-led movements such as Fight for $15 for years. In response to corporations making insincere claims and not responding to the needs of restaurant workers, in July of 2020 fast-food work stoppages across the nation took place in support of the Strike for Black Lives (Saxena 2020). Fast-food workers are the vanguard of this movement as they organize workers across the nation, sign petitions for hazard pay, strike, and lead the charge in increasing the federal minimum wage. Similar to workers across the food system, like the Teamsters at Hunts Point Produce Market Workers' Union striking to the first Instacart

Figure 11.1 Burgerville's Allies for Change sign, July 2020 (Whitney Shervey).

Figure 11.2 Chicago McDonald's workers on strike (Brusky 2020).

union in Illinois, to grocery store workers enduring the ongoing battle with hazard pay, the organizing of restaurant workers is a direct reaction to the conditions workers are experiencing while working during the COVID-19 pandemic (Figure 11.2).

COVID-19 has pushed restaurant workers to their boiling point, creating optimal conditions for unprecedented organizing in the workplace. Since the historical unionizing of the Burgerville Workers Union in Portland, Oregon in 2018, other restaurant workers have been organizing and unionizing. This precedent has given restaurant workers actionable ways to address inequities in the workplace through worker power. During the pandemic, the Burgerville Workers Union is using their power to challenge inadequate responses to address COVID-19 by their employers (Food Chain Workers Alliance 2021: 22). Other workers are organizing for the first time and are confronting their employers' racism. Hailing from the tourist destination Voodoo Doughnuts in Portland, Oregon, Doughnut Workers United began their organizing efforts in 2020 and are asking for Voodoo Doughnuts to not only recognize their union but also change their racist business name. Unionized restaurant workers have the leverage to challenge workplace safety during COVID-19, yet their ability to hold their employers accountable when they are making hollow

Figure 11.3 Doughnut Workers United on the picket line, July 2020 (Whitney Shervey).

claims to address structural racism needs the support of their customer base (Figure 11.3).

In the age of COVID-19, more than ever convenience has become a priority for eaters and that convenience comes with a cost. From the fast-food drive-through to the delivery services of the gig economy, COVID-19 has strengthened consumer relationships with convenience. This convenience is made possible by structural racism that disproportionately impacts women of color. Whether you are relying on restaurant workers or delivery drivers to keep you fed or are another worker in the food system, I urge you to look beyond the statements coming from the top and find solidarity in worker-led movements. Fast-food chains already have a platform and do not need their voices amplified. So, the next time you see them making claims on their social media, think twice before pressing the "Like" button.

My task is to ask all of you to take it upon yourself to know what workers are already doing to address inequality in their workplace. I ask you to trust the experiences of the workers and hold corporations accountable when they are making sweeping claims of how they plan to address racism. I also ask you to reflect on what solidarity means to you. To me, solidarity means showing up knowing that the struggle of the folks you are showing up for is your struggle. It is the role of white people to figure out how your struggle intersects with Black Lives Matter and to show up. It is the role of customers to figure out how your struggle intersects with restaurant workers and show up.

Please, show up!

References

Brusky, J. (2020) 'Fight for $15 Show Us Black Lives Matter.' *image, Flickr*, Available July 24, 2020 at: https://www.flickr.com/photos/40969298@N05/50025996817/

CDC (Centers for Disease Control and Prevention) (2021) *COVID-19 Hospitalization and Death by Race/Ethnicity*. Atlanta, GA: National Center for Immunization and Respiratory Diseases Division of Viral Diseases. Available at: https://www.cdc.gov/coronavirus/2019-ncov/covid-data/investigations-discovery/hospitalization-death-by-race-ethnicity.html [Accessed: 2.14.21].

Chen, Y.H., Glymour, M., Riley, A., Balmes, J., Duchowny, K., Harrison, R., Matthay, E. and Bibbins-Domingo, K. (2021) *Excess Mortality Associated with the COVID-19 Pandemic Among Californians 18-65 Years of Age, by Occupational Sector and Occupation: March through October 2020*. medRxiv. Available at: https://www.medrxiv.org/content/10.1101/2021.01.21.21250266v1.full.pdf [Accessed 2.14.21].

Entmacher, J., Frohlich, L., Robbins, K.G., Martin, E. and Watson, L. (2014) *Underpaid and Overloaded: Women in Low-wage Jobs*. Washington, DC: National Women's Law Center. Available at: https://nwlc.org/wp-content/uploads/2015/08/final_nwlc_lowwagereport2014.pdf [Accessed 2.14.21].

Food Chain Workers Alliance (2021) *We are Not Disposable, Food Workers Organizing on the Covid Frontlines*. Los Angeles, CA: Food Chain Workers Alliance. Available at: https://foodchainworkers.org/wp-content/uploads/2021/02/Food-Workers-Organizing-on-the-COVID-Frontlines-FINAL.pdf [Accessed 2.28.21].

Frane, A. (2021) 'With No Clear Vaccination Plan, Portland Restaurant Workers Are Uneasy About Indoor Dining.' Eater Portland, OR. 2.12.21. Available at: https://pdx.eater.com/2021/2/12/22277096/portland-indoor-dining [Accessed 2.20.21].

Lo, J. and Oliva, J. (2020) 'Food workers versus Food Giants.' In Jayaraman, S. and De Master, K. (eds.) *Bite Back: People Taking on Corporate Food and Winning.* Berkeley, CA: UC Press. pp. 99–106.

Nittle, N. (2020) 'People of Color are at Greater Risk of COVID-19. Systemic Racism in the Food System Plays a Role.' Civil Eats. 5.5.20. Available at: https://civileats.com/2020/05/05/people-of-color-are-at-greater-risk-of-covid-19 -systemic-racism-in-the-food-system-plays-a-role/ [Accessed 2.20.21].

Reyes, T., Benner, C. and Jayaraman, S. (2015) *Ending Jim Crow in America's Restaurants: Racial and Gender Occupational Segregation in the Restaurant Industry.* New York, NY: Restaurant Opportunities Center United. Available at: https://chapters.rocunited.org/wp-content/uploads/2015/10/RaceGender_Report _LR.pdf [Accessed 2.14.21].

Saxena, J. (2020) 'Food workers Across the Country Join the Strike for Black Lives.' Eater. 7.20.20. Available at: https://www.eater.com/2020/7/20/21331616 /food-workers-strike-for-black-lives [Accessed 2.21.21].

Sharma, D. (2021) 'The True Cost of Convenience.' Eater. 1.22.21. Available at: https://www.eater.com/22228352/convenience-of-delivery-apps-destroying -restaurants-uber-eats-doordash-postmates [Accessed 2.21.21].

Waxman, N. (2020) 'Chicago Fast-Food workers Say Companies Aren't Protecting Them From COVID-19.' Eater Chicago. 6.10.20. Available at: https://chicago. eater.com/2020/6/10/21285361/taco-bell-mcdonalds-workers-protest-coronvirus-covid-19-restaurant-worker-sues-grubhub-chicago [Accessed 2.20.21].

Part 4

Beyond COVID: moving forward with policy and research

12 COVID-19 and feminist methods: one year later[1]

Ann R. Tickamyer

A year into the COVID-19 pandemic, with new hope but no clear end point, lessons for gender researchers have become both more obvious and more frustrating. From the beginning, COVID-19 visibly functioned as a giant sorting mechanism. In the United States, early reports highlighted that it separated the young from the old, women from men, the healthy from the at-risk, those deemed in essential services from the rest of the work-force, the homed from the homeless, the urban from the rural, even the right from the left. Most of all, but largely unsaid, it divides the privileged from the poor and marginalized. Fundamental social cleavages are deeply implicated in who is most vulnerable, how the virus is spread, what are the consequences, and what recovery might look like. The usual suspects of gender, race, ethnicity, age, sexuality, and class figure prominently and urgently. Every source of information, whether from researchers, journalists, or friends and family, underscores the relevance and necessity of deep dives into intersectional analysis based on demographic, social, and spatial locations. These sources also highlight the obstacles to this approach and the ensuing costs to research and policy for gender analysis, following the precepts of feminist theory and epistemology.[2]

Although no surprise to gender researchers, for many observers COVID-19 has been a wakeup call on society's dependence on and the precarity of women's work in a deeply and systemically unequal gendered division of labor. Whether paid or unpaid but too often invisible and devalued, women's work features prominently both as providers and targets. Women disproportionately work in the service industries where they are either deemed essential or are out of a job – health care workers and cleaners on the one hand, restaurant servers and retail workers on the other – and some fall in between, such as teachers and day care providers whose services are variously defined as essential or not, as the political winds blow. They are agricultural workers in an industry that remains stereotyped as male. At home they are the primary care takers with the normal heavy responsibilities

DOI: 10.4324/9781003198277-16

multiplied during social isolation. The vulnerabilities and burdens are magnified when race and class are added to the mix. Documenting these and the numerous other inequities of the pandemic is critical to better understanding the many differential impacts buried in the rhetoric of a "pandemic" that in principle affects everyone equally but actually varies widely. Yet in a cruel irony, it is harder than ever to accomplish this work.

The situation is deeply frustrating because it embodies a contradiction. At a time when we need additional, rigorous, and in-depth research into the intersectional gendered impacts of global disaster, it has been difficult-to-impossible to conduct direct research on what is happening in the field. The activities necessary to continue many research projects, both COVID-19 and non-COVID-19 related, are in direct contravention to safety requirements, restrictions imposed by sponsoring institutions, and basic common sense. It has been impossible to travel, to interview, to observe, and document in person what is happening, and even if it were possible, it would defy fundamental ethical obligations to the participants of such study. The more remote the location or the fewer the resources available to the community, the more important it is to understand and document the realities on the ground, but the greater the barriers to doing so. The first obligation of any research is to do no harm, and in ordinary circumstances with reasonable precautions and observance of human subject protocols, that is not an issue. But in the case of a worldwide pandemic, any effort must be regarded as a potential harm to be avoided until safety can be assured for participants, researchers, and their respective communities. We need to hear diverse voices, perspectives, and experiences, and as researchers we need to facilitate their dissemination. During the pandemic, up to the time of writing and for the foreseeable future, this has been difficult and, in many cases, impossible.

A case in point: on March 1, 2020, I returned home to State College, Pennsylvania, from a scoping trip in Dillingham Alaska for collaborators on a large transdisciplinary research project on the impacts of climate change in coastal Alaskan communities. The spread of coronavirus in the United States was just becoming obvious, and we were glad to get home, although its extent and impacts were only starting to be experienced. A few short weeks later, we went into "lockdown" mode, sheltering in place "to flatten the curve" of its transmission. The curve resisted flattening, climbing ever higher amid controversy over appropriate public health measures, while project team members, university faculty, and members of the larger population with the luxury of maintaining distance and belief in science withdrew from all but virtual social contact. As we practiced social isolation, many remote Alaskan villages, remembering the devastation brought by past epidemics, practiced entire community isolation, restricting access

Figure 12.1 Community activism in Dillingham, Alaska (Ann R. Tickamyer).

to outsiders; others struggled with the consequences of lacking that control; both modes with implications for health, safety, and food security (Figures 12.1 and 12.2).

The trip to Alaska was to be the first to different coastal communities particularly threatened by rising temperatures to establish relations, trust, access, communication, and permission for future research on the complex

Figure 12.2 Community activism in Dillingham parade (Ann R. Tickamyer).

connections between food security, migration, and climate change in the Arctic and its gendered practices and consequences. Polar regions are experiencing warming at a much higher rate than more temperate locations. Tribal and indigenous communities heavily depend on subsistence activities for food security, sovereignty, and cultural continuity that are threatened by climate change. The purpose of our research is to document and analyze the links between rising temperatures, threats to infrastructure, and individual, family, and community impacts and responses. This work requires the cooperation and participation of the communities in question, but that entails building trust and avenues of communication. Many tribal communities, remembering the devastation brought by past incursions of Western authorities and the diseases and dislocations they introduced, carefully guard prerogatives to determine with whom and when to participate in research projects. Many also have relatively few resources to connect virtually through broadband access. The ubiquitous Zoom meetings of academic life during the pandemic are alien to locations with absent, limited, or expensive connectivity. Access was already a high hurdle; now it has been deferred with no clear path to when and how it can be established or resumed. As the lone gender researcher on the project, this is particularly distressing given how few studies on this topic have used a gendered lens.

Research around the world repeats this scenario. Many projects have shut down or gone on hiatus, with no clear time frame for resumption. In some places preestablished relationships and ongoing data collection by local researchers continue either directly or virtually, but in many cases it has been suspended or radically transformed. Where possible, phone, video, and mail substitute for field research, but often with deep compromise in the nature and quality of the data amid many limits to the reach of virtual communication methods. Even in the United States, large segments of rural populations have little access to broadband and wireless communications. Remote portions of Alaska surrounded by wilderness are by no means the only example. In my state of Pennsylvania, it is estimated that somewhere between a third to one half of residents lack connectivity, primarily in rural areas and among low-income households (Meinrath et al. 2019), and this is repeated across the country. Worldwide, the more marginalized the group, the more likely they are to have limited or no access. Furthermore, the greater the gender inequality, the less likely women will have access to the Internet or freedom to participate in a research study, even if there is community or household access. Researchers worry that efforts to talk to women in problematic settings will spark distrust and even violence. Many reports from around the world suggest an increase in family violence from the loss of livelihoods and the isolation measures advocated for virus protection. This situation desperately requires serious inquiry and research to determine the extent of the problem. Researchers and activists attempting to reach women in isolated households, especially in highly patriarchal and sex-segregated communities and cultures require great ingenuity to ascertain whether women are free to speak but have little recourse when denied except taking care to keep their research from creating suspicion or exacerbating vulnerabilities.

What is to be done? There are few easy answers. I have previously advocated for better attention to how well feminist ideals in research are put into practice. As illustrated by multiple pieces in this volume, the first step is to ensure that data collection and analysis are disaggregated by sex. This best practice remains far from universal, including most recently in COVID-19 reports and studies. We know that rural food and agricultural workers have been hard-hit by the virus. Some of the earliest reports indicated disruption of the food supply from outbreaks in food processing plants and among field workers. We also know that men and women experience the disease differently, possibly at different rates, and with different recovery times and processes. We do not know how these and other gender differences manifest among food and agricultural workers. The data may exist but have not been widely disseminated. This is also a lesson in the importance of remembering that a gender lens includes men and masculinities and nonbinary gender identification as critical areas for research.

Beyond that basic step, participatory methods become a critically important practice, particularly, moving beyond advocacy to an actuality. This is primarily appropriate in fieldwork, one of the reasons why qualitative methods feature so prominently in feminist methodology, but opportunities for meaningful participation should be evaluated for all forms of data collection. Here, too, the ethical and the practical coincide. Potentially, this can enable easier continuation of research by local collaborators even where outside researchers lose access. It is not a solution but moves in the right direction.

Case in point 2: long before the Alaskan research, I have been a collaborator on research on gender roles, ideology, and practices in Indonesia, and how these relate to resilience in disaster (Tickamyer and Kusujiarti 2020). The summer of 2020 was to include a trip to Indonesia to consult with colleagues there and to conduct follow-up research, a plan upended by the pandemic. Fortunately, work continues, although not necessarily as we had planned, because of the ongoing collaboration with local researchers and their experience conducting participatory research. Of course, like the rest of the world, health and safety restrictions and precautions hamper their work, but to the extent possible, it continues (Figure 12.3).

Sex-disaggregated data is the tip of the iceberg. Intersectional analysis requires more extensive demographic data on relevant social locations.

Figure 12.3 Feminist methods workshop in Indonesia (Ann R. Tickamyer).

US food and agricultural workers again illustrate. Very large proportions of these workforces are race and ethnic minorities, often located in rural areas, often immigrants, sometimes undocumented, and invariably low-income. Diligent efforts by journalists to ferret out news about the pandemic have made it clear that these are among the populations who have experienced the most devastation from COVID-19, with high incidence of infection, morbidity, and mortality. It should not be necessary to rely on piecing together news items from around the country, however rigorously investigated, to see a complete picture of disease disparities. Even with the highest standards, news accounts are not likely to have the rigor of social-science-directed investigation or to use the same frameworks. For example, feminist scholars and practitioners applying an intersectional framework need to think carefully about the categories necessary for the analysis both generally and in the specific case. These are not static nor predefined but must be applied in conjunction with context in mind.

Another important step in line with feminist methodology requires practicing reflexivity and introspection. Lia Bryant's chapter in this volume describes autoethnography: writing memories of persons, places, events, and interactions in the third person to stimulate deeper understanding of their meaning and significance. As a researcher grounded and barred from making new observations in the field, such work strengthens powers of reflection, creating new "muscles" of introspection that enhance insight and even lead to new avenues of inquiry. Social isolation, working from home, increased self-provisioning and care work, reliance on Zoom and other forms of technology, and always the threat of disease and illness, are conducive to forming new research questions about how these factors unfold and are experienced in the lives of both the researcher and their subjects. As difficult as it has been from a position of relative privilege, one can only imagine the hardships experienced by those with fewer resources, but it is incumbent on us to do so. It also is necessary to advocate for support and change. Many of the chapters in this book detail the increased burdens of care and precarity that have fallen to women with little respite or assistance. While forms, sources, and amounts of support vary around the world, in most places they have been woefully inadequate, exacerbating gender inequities, and putting the onus on individual women and families to cope. Transformational change requires collective action.

Finally, feminist and gender scholars must take every opportunity to highlight inequalities with research designed to uncover power dynamics and differentials to advocate for women's empowerment and gender transformation in agriculture, food production, and beyond. This is particularly apropos at a time when the realities of pandemic vulnerabilities and inequities intersect with those occasioned by the pain and violence of police brutality, institutional and individual racism, and growing inability to hide from the realities of the cruelties and oppression experienced by persons of color on the one hand and various forms of white privilege on the other. This is true from my vantage point in the United States, but also applies globally where gender, race, ethnicity, and nationality targeted forms of violence and deprivation taken separately and together are no strangers to people's lives. Protest has spread from the United States to become a global movement. Pandemic social isolation has not spared us scenes of horrifying violence ranging from mass shootings in the United States to attacks on democratic institutions and demonstrators in the United States and Myanmar. Less shocking but equally disturbing, disasters, both natural and human-induced, continue to damage lives and livelihoods with floods, famine, fire, and plague that also have intersectionality-defined differences in vulnerabilities, impacts, and outcomes.

Many pundits speculate on what life will look like if and when we emerge on the other side of these intertwined disasters. It is incumbent on feminist researchers to be prepared to study, participate, and help shape the new reality.

Notes

1 This research was supported in part by the National Science Foundation (Award # ICER-1927827).
2 See Tickamyer and Sexsmith (2019) and Tickamyer (2020) for descriptions and discussions of feminist methodology.

References

Meinrath, S., with H. Bonestroo, G. Bullen, A. Jansen, S. Mansour, C. Mitchell, C. Ritzo, and N. Thieme. (2019). *Broadband Availability and Access in Rural Pennsylvania*. Harrisburg, PA: Center for Rural Pennsylvania. Accessed March 24, 2021 at https://www.rural.palegislature.us/broadband/Broadband_Availability_and_Access_in_Rural_Pennsylvania_2019_Report.pdf

Tickamyer, A.R. (2020). "Feminist Methods and Methodology in Agricultural Research." In C. Sachs, L. Jensen, K. Sexsmith, and P. Castellanos (eds.), *Gender and Agriculture Handbook*. NY: Taylor and Francis/Routledge.

Tickamyer, A.R., and S. Kusujiarti. (2020). "Riskscapes of Gender, Disaster, and Climate Change in Indonesia." *Cambridge Journal of Regions, Economy, and Society* 13, 233–251.

Tickamyer, A.R., and Sexsmith, K. (2019). "How to Do Gender Research? Feminist Perspectives on Gender Research in Agriculture." In C. Sachs (ed.), *Gender, Agriculture and Agrarian Transformations*. New York: Routledge, 57–71.

13 The importance of sex-disaggregated and gender data to a gender-inclusive COVID-19 response in the aquatic food systems

Afrina Choudhury, Surendran Rajaratnam, and Cynthia McDougall

Sex-disaggregated data and gender data are central to making informed policy and development program decisions for people reliant on the fisheries and aquaculture sector. Data collected and analyzed separately on males and females can be defined as sex-disaggregated data (Doss and Kieran 2014). In addition to collection and presentation of data by sex, gender data also reflects gender issues, is based on concepts and definitions that consider the diversity of women and men and all aspects of their lives, and is developed through collection methods that take into account stereotypes and social and cultural factors that may induce bias in data (United Nations Department of Economic and Social Affairs, 2016). Although sex-disaggregated data provides basic information by sex, policies and programs need gender data – including about barriers – in order to be inclusive and effective. Despite their significance, sex-disaggregated data (SDD) and gender data (GD) are not systematically collected and are lacking worldwide. This was problematic before COVID-19 and has been exacerbated with the onset of the global pandemic. Governments, as well as development and civil society organizations, are working to tackle the disastrous economic and social repercussions of the pandemic and its restrictions. Yet, these efforts are – often unknowingly – undermined by the lack of recognition and data about gender barriers and the different needs, resilience, and relative risks to people of all genders. Persistent gender data gaps, in other words, limit understanding about gendered differences – and the intersecting factors of poverty, caste, ethnicity, legal, or other status such as lack of legal citizenship. This limitation, in turn, significantly undermines the ability of policy and programming to work for the people who need it the most.

This challenge is critical in the fisheries and aquaculture sectors, notably in relation to understanding and responding to the gendered and diverse

DOI: 10.4324/9781003198277-17

needs of small-scale and informal fishers, processors, and retailers. Women play major roles in, and make significant contributions to, the fisheries and aquaculture sector worldwide, but these mostly remain unrecognized, from individual households to the scale of policy. The lack of recognition includes the fact that women's contributions are often reframed as "supporting roles" to "men's work" in a sector that is seen as a male domain (Kleiber et al. 2015; Harper et al. 2020). In this chapter, we explore the need for sex-disaggregated and gender data through examples from the highly fisheries and aquaculture-dependent contexts of India and Bangladesh. In particular, we present COVID-19-related challenges and responses that have gendered implications and highlight the importance of sex-disaggregated data and gender data to understand and cushion the (intersectionally) gendered impacts of the pandemic in the fisheries and aquaculture.

Insights from Bangladesh and India

In Bangladesh, despite the perception of the sector as a male domain, almost 80 percent of the workforce in fish and shrimp processing factories and drying sites are women and young children (Belton et al. 2014). However, these women are predominantly employed in low-level positions, with low-income and inadequate safety standards and hygiene in place (Choudhury et al. 2017). When COVID-19 hit Bangladesh, the lockdown issued by the government drastically reduced orders, fish landings, and supplies in general. Most of these plants and drying sites either shut down or significantly reduced operations, leaving thousands of women workers jobless and with few alternatives.

Furthermore, return migration of men from the city and other regions (as a result of job loss) added extra pressure on the fishing labor market in Bangladesh. Increasing numbers of men are thus now engaging in areas on which women relied for their livelihoods pre-pandemic, such as shore-based fishing and gleaning resulting in reduced catches for these women fishers. The lack of livelihood opportunities for women, and threats to existing ones, led women to use their existing stocks of dried fish, thereby depleting their source of income and food without being able to replace it. Even with a decrease in fish prices in the market, many women could not afford to purchase fish because they could not generate the required income during the initial period of the pandemic. To combat livelihood losses, the Government of Bangladesh has continued to issue rations to registered fishers – "registered" being the key word here. Women in Bangladesh are not recognized as fishers, and thus not registered as fishers. As a consequence, women are therefore unable to access these rations. Unfortunately, policy definitions of "fishers" exclude people involved in post-harvest parts of the value chain as well as those involved in gleaning, which is where women are primarily involved. Therefore, dry-fish producers (including women), laborers in processing plants and drying sites (mostly women), have no "fisher" identification cards, hence they do not get the needed support from the government. The narrow and arguably gendered definition in the sector results in this COVID-19 social protection measure being inaccessible to many people who need it the most.

In Assam, India, a study we conducted in communities reliant on pond aquaculture and *beel* (floodplain wetlands) fisheries found women taking primary responsibility for reproductive activities such as food preparation. In some communities they are also involved in dry- and fermented fish production. At the same time, however, members of the household (including women) conform to inequitable gender norms regarding intra-household food distribution. Women tend to eat only after serving other family members. Their reproductive work is unpaid and little recognized or valued (even when it contributes to household income). The initial state-wide COVID-19 lockdown imposed by the government that affected the income and food supply of households was worst for poor households who do not have adequate amounts of food stocked. Women in this lower socioeconomic group and families are likely to be especially heavily impacted by this inadequacy and the low quality of food given the pre-existing inequitable norms. Even with food assistance given by government and non-government agencies, failure to understand and address gendered intra-household food allocation can cause the deterioration of women's nutrition and health. Moreover, this has intergenerational consequences: undermining the nutrition of women of reproduction age directly undermines nutrition essential in the first 1,000 days of life, affecting the development of unborn children and infants.

In the state of Odisha, a key entry point for many women in (otherwise male-dominated) aquaculture production is through state-sponsored women's groups. These groups aim to contribute to women's economic empowerment through fish production and marketing. COVID-19, however, led to members being unable to purchase fish feed and other pond maintenance products due to restrictions in transportation/mobility and the closure of shops. Fingerlings were not available at the right time; therefore the stocking of the fingerlings was affected/delayed. The women's groups also faced challenges to harvesting fish from their fish ponds due to unavailability of men to do the work (a constraint that highlights the continuing strongly gendered norms and division of labor in this context). The groups were also less able to market the fish due to restrictions in transportation/mobility. An additional insight from Odisha is that although both women and men access reservoirs to fish, and the challenges faced by women and men fishers were reported to be similar, women cope with the economic impact of COVID-19 in a way that men did not. Specifically, women utilized their home gardens to plant and cultivate vegetables. This helped to reduce their purchase of vegetables from the market, which had increased in price, thus keeping their expenses low. Women also expanded on their small home-based businesses during COVID-19, including marketing homemade snacks such as papads and pickles as well as making fabric face masks for local sale.

Similar to the situation in Bangladesh, the return migration of men who left to work in the city or other states impacted the livelihoods of resident women and men in their communities in India. Although the return of (now unemployed) young men in aquaculture and fisheries may create new opportunities, it may also displace women and less powerful men who are barely surviving the economic challenges brought by the pandemic. Even with cross-state borders opening again, the number of men migrating out of Assam's fishing communities again to work is reported to be less than previously. This could mean that competition for work within the fishing community work may continue to be higher than pre-pandemic.

In both Assam and Odisha, as with many other contexts, women are heavily dependent on the post-harvest part of fish value chains and so were particularly affected by changes in markets. In Assam, women who earn income as fish processors reported being affected by lockdown and movement restrictions. These COVID-19 controls also affected women who relied on fish pickle and fermented fish production, because of the downturn on special events and celebrations. Women's income from fish drying was also affected as these products couldn't be sent to neighboring states, which is its normal market. In Odisha, women selling fish from their homestead ponds reported that the price of fish went down during the initial phase of travel restrictions as these fish were unable to be sold in the market. Similarly, women selling fish at farm gate reported a 25 percent drop in volume.

The need for sex-disaggregated and gender data

Despite the aquatic food sector being considered a male domain (a perception due in part to the lack of sex-disaggregated and gender data), women as well as men depend on and contribute to the sector. However, as illustrated in this chapter, they may be affected differently by shocks. This underscores the need to make informed policy and development program decisions based on sex-disaggregated data and gender data for the sector to thrive and benefit women and men equally. In conjunction with this, policy, development, private sector and research actors need to rethink "what counts" as fisheries – directly affecting "who is counted." Women's engagement in, their contributions to, and the gender barriers that persist in the fisheries and aquaculture sector need to be identified, measured, and addressed in government and non-government responses. This is imperative now in relation to the COVID-19 pandemic and also in relation to climate change and future shocks as well.

In this complex time, WorldFish and partners have conducted a range of studies to understand the impacts of COVID-19 on the fisheries and aquaculture sector. With the large number of unrecognized, unreported women working in the lower and informal rungs of aquatic foods chains or in small-scale production, we found that even getting teams to effectively sample and engage equally and representatively with women has proven to be challenging. Even women business owners and entrepreneurs who are working in the sector, and women who play key roles in small (household) businesses, remain un- or under-recognized and reported, and thus underrepresented in insights from research. This is compounded by the increased work burdens women are facing in many contexts. Moreover, due to gendered access to phones and constraining norms, COVID-19 pandemic's social distancing guidelines and resultant phone interviews mean that women's inputs may be further at a risk unless special measures are taken. To try to counter these risks, WorldFish, together with ACIAR, produced tips on gender integration in research during COVID-19 (see McDougall and Curnow 2020). WorldFish also generated a guidance note on research quality during distance research that explicitly recognizes gender integration as central to quality (McDougall et al. 2020).

Given the high populations and population densities in India and Bangladesh, the multiple challenges people face in accessing and benefiting from the health care services, the loss of livelihood and income and many other challenges the disease brought to the countries, the impact of COVID-19 may be far worse than what is being reported. These impacts are gendered, with women and girls bearing the brunt and often not receiving the needed support to overcome the challenges brought by the pandemic. With persisting gender gaps in access to inputs and resources already, we need to take extra precautions to ensure the COVID-19 response is at a minimum gender-responsive, if not transformative (see McDougall et al. 2015). Gender data gaps lead to gender-blind policies and frameworks, but also to implementation of responses to shocks that may exclude women from the safety nets, support, and investments that are much needed for an inclusive recovery and for building forward better.

Continuing our work given COVID-19 restrictions and risks

Surendran Rajaratnam

When the threats of the COVID-19 pandemic were announced by the Malaysian government in early 2020, we prepared to work from home for a short period of time initially. Little did I know that the temporary change would still remain, a year later. Having to change the way I work was challenging in the beginning as I try not to bring work back home. However, over the past year, I managed to adapt to this new work arrangement. An amount of field work planned in India early last year couldn't be conducted due to the travel restrictions. One plan for a study was changed to a desk-based study as we couldn't foresee the end of the travel restrictions last year. Studies which were able to be conducted remotely continued with the support of field-based staffs and partners. These were conducted by following the country's procedures and taking precautions to ensure that our work doesn't risk the staff as well as people in the community.

Cynthia McDougall

In terms of field work, the major adaptation to COVID-19 was about shifting to virtual methods. While this posed challenges, it has also pushed us to be creative – such as teams and participants figuring out how to use WhatsApp to share inputs. One positive aspect for which I am grateful is that the challenges also created opportunities for transdisciplinary partnerships that had not existed previously. In a sense, we partners found each other through the need to rapidly learn and share lessons about what works for different women and men in these incredibly difficult times. At a personal level, the family all working and schooling from home in Penang, Malaysia, took some adjustments, but I would not trade that time together for anything. It has been an important prompt to reassess work–life balance and quality of life.

Afrina Choudhury

During the COVID-19 outbreak in early 2020, I was in the Wageningen University & Research (WUR) as a PhD student. As my PhD study is partially funded by WorldFish, I also spend a few hours every week managing some of the projects of the organization in Bangladesh. I was lucky to be able to board the last flight out of Amsterdam to Vancouver to join my husband as the preparation for state-wide lockdown was in place. I have been working from home since then, attending classes online, completing assignments. I have been managing these responsibilities on top of my pregnancy, childbirth, and childcare.

Acknowledgments

This work was undertaken as part of the CGIAR Research Program on Fish Agri-Food Systems (FISH) led by WorldFish. The program is supported by contributors to the CGIAR trust fund. The chapter benefited from data provided by WorldFish and partners in Odisha and Assam, India, and in Bangladesh.

References

Belton, B., Hossain, A.R.M., Rahman, M. & Thilsted, S.H., 2014. Dried -fish production, consumption and trade in Bangladesh. *In*: S.H. Thilsted & M.A. Wahab, eds. *World Bank/SAFANSI Funded Regional Workshop on Small Fish and Nutrition*, 1-2 March, 2014 Dhaka.

Bennett, N.J., *et al.*, 2020. The COVID-19 pandemic, small-scale fisheries and coastal fishing communities. *Coastal Management*, 48(4), 336–347.

Choudhury, A., McDougall, C., Rajaratnam, S. & Park, C.M.Y., 2017. *Women's Empowerment in Aquaculture: Two Case Studies from Bangladesh*. Rome: Food and Agriculture Organisation of the United Nations; Penang: WorldFish.

Doss, C. & Kieran, C. 2014. Three things you need to know about sex-disaggregated data. Available from: https://a4nh.cgiar.org/2014/05/05/three-things-you-need-to-know-about-sex-disaggregated-data/

Harper, S., *et al.*, 2020. Valuing invisible catches: Estimating the global contribution by women to small-scale marine capture fisheries production. *PLoS ONE*, 15(3), 1–16.

Kleiber, D., Harris, L.M. & Vincent, A.C., 2015. Gender and small-scale fisheries: A case for counting women and beyond. *Fish and Fisheries*, 16(4), 547–562.

McDougall, C. & Curnow, J., 2020. Safeguarding gender integration in research during the COVID-19 pandemic. Retrieved from https://pim.cgiar.org/2020/05/29/safeguarding-gender-integration-in-research-during-the-covid-19-pandemic/

McDougall, C., *et al.*, 2015. Implementing a gender transformative research approach: early lessons. *In*: CRP AAS. *Research in Development: Learning from the CGIAR Research Program on Aquatic Agricultural Systems*. Penang: WorldFish.

McDougall, C., *et al.*, 2020. Ten strategies for research quality in distance research during COVID-19 and future food system shocks.

United Nations Department of Economic and Social Affairs, 2016. Integrating a gender perspective into statistics. *Studies in Methods*, Series F No.111. Available from https://unstats.un.org/unsd/demographic-social/Standards-and-Methods/files/Handbooks/gender/Integrating-a-Gender-Perspective-into-Statistics-E.pdf

14 In and out of place

Lia Bryant

Introduction

> She stares at yellow fields of wheat flicking past her. The long stretch of road ahead. Feeling the rhythm and dip of the car as she manoeuvres around corners, she notices the size and shape of trees dotted along the open spaces. She holds a conversation with herself; it's almost a game identifying crops by their growth and color (Figure 14.1).

For a qualitative researcher like me, rural research is very much emplaced and sensory. COVID-19 physically removes me from the communities and rural people I partner with and I am increasingly on my mobile phone. On days when the Internet is good (it often isn't in rural Australia), I am on Zoom. My work now involves sitting in my home office in suburban Adelaide, South Australia. I now listen carefully to voices. However, so much of what I have learned about rurality and gender emerged from being in place and, a lot of the time, it's from being there but feeling out of place.

Paradoxically, it is in the city where I have often reflected back on rural places using memory work, an auto-ethnographic method which involves the writing of a memory in the third person on an encounter, emotion, or theme. As memory work enables me to be reflexive about my practice it made sense while being physically away from the rural to use this method for writing this piece (see Bryant and Livholts, 2007, 2015).

Out of place: matter that matters

I enjoy thinking about how the spaces I enter hold histories and take shape materially in bricks and mortar. I am curious about how spaces come alive through language but also through our senses as people enter a local grocery shop in a rural town, a farm house, a shearing shed, and paddocks. Particularly, I am interested in how we affect one another and how we are

DOI: 10.4324/9781003198277-18

Figure 14.1 Wheat (Lia Bryant).

affected by objects, landscapes, insects, elements, and animals. These entangled affective relationships have occupied social scholarship for some time and feminist theorists (Butler, 1993; Haraway, 1988, 2008; Barad, 2003) have brought attention to a focus on women's bodies in relation to "things."

Hence, I dedicated a chapter, "Sites/sights of exclusion," in my book *Water and Rural Communities* to the colonial structure of the water-governance building. I bring attention to the white masculinised board room where large heavy portraits of chairmen of the board hang (Bryant and George, 2016). In the board room, the power of "things" becomes apparent – a table, chairs, portraits of men, and cabinets of tools many of which are unknown to me. This building is not simply a representation of the past. It is matter

Figure 14.2 The Boardroom of the Water Trust (Lia Bryant).

that matters. The textures of the Water Trust's built environment are "felt materially and atmospheric attunements are palpable and sensory" (Tolia Kelly, 2011:157, citing Stewart, 2011:446). This living space (Jacobs, 2006) endorses a political praxis of welcoming some bodies over others (Figure 14.2).

I have a vivid memory of my first visit to the Trust: I was ushered in to sit in high dark wooden chairs along a table that was equally heavy and ornate. I remember thinking this room was reminiscent of a dining hall in an English castle. The furniture was obviously imported when the town was settled – erasing the presence of Indigenous Australians and the waves of non-British migration since 1950. I noted the sensations of discomfort growing as my body was forced upright in this formal setting. It was hard to make eye contact with the men who sat up and down the length of the table. I came to talk about gender and water governance during drought.

At one point in the discussion I asked, "Are there women on the board of the Water Trust?"

I was met with throaty laughter. "In our 120 years, we haven't had a woman on the board."

My body in this space was foreign and I felt it and wondered how a woman (or eventually women) might feel if they were able to navigate a seat at this table. With COVID-19 requiring a greater reliance on Zoom for meetings it is unclear whether this has resulted in inequalities becoming further entrenched as fewer new people are inducted into governance or has access to meetings from home opened up space for women's participation?

In place: farm women make place matter

I often wonder "how do those bodies absented from place leave their mark?"

As the Water Trust example shows, especially for rural and farming women, their impact is sometimes erased; while strong in the fabric of history, their mark is often grainy like the layered and discernible strands of stringy bark on the trunk of a gumtree.

Having spoken to farming and rural women over the courses of many research projects I have many memories of the hard, often undervalued, work women undertake on- and off-farm (Bryant and Pini, 2011). An interview with Sophie stays with me as her work is often unacknowledged as farm labor in official statistics but her presence provides the rhythm for ongoing production. I came to Sophie's farm to interview her about her experiences of being pluriactive (farming and working off-farm) and recall:

> The house was new but not. The floors were concrete and the walls plastered but unpainted. There were big windows in the living room facing the long stretches of paddocks where you could see stumpy growth – cabbages I think. Sophie explained how she had been on night shift packing fruit and veg for a corporate farm. She said she took the night shift so she could be home to get the kids to school then collect them after school. But she also needed to work on-farm especially during harvest. There was only so much they could pay out for farm workers. For Sophie the unpainted walls and lack of soft furnishings were too much to think about. She told me "you know I just don't care about …" [waving her hand around the room]. I looked into her eyes and I could read her exhaustion.

In Australia due to COVID-19, farming women are undertaking more labor. In horticulture, for example, women's hours on-farm have become longer as temporary visas for overseas farm workers have been halted, and during snap lockdowns women with school-aged children are doing more domestic work and home schooling. However, the pandemic has come at a time when other disasters are impacting rural Australia – a recent prolonged drought, devasting bushfires and severe floods, as well as the financial consequences of international trade disputes. What is yet to be known is how climatic disaster, COVID-19, and the political economy have impacted on farming women's socio-economic activities and overall health. Research *in place* is now necessary to feel and sense the textures of altered landscapes and altered lives.

In place and out of place: missing the textures of gender politics

By entering the rural as a researcher residing in a city, I have had the opportunity to grapple with the textures of gender politics in place alongside my own gender politics. My memory below reveals body politics in place or the gendering of space in the act of becoming:

> She had to go to Mudamuckla. There were no maps and she relied on directions taken from a telephone call. She drove the government car down dirt roads where no buildings or humans were in sight. In the vastness she felt vulnerable and uncertain. Too much space. She saw a shed – could this be the landmark where she was told she must turn right? Again isolation and uncertainty. Deciding to turn right she drove down a narrow dirt path seemingly leading nowhere. Go on or turn back? Well she did go on and found herself in a paddock surrounded by cows. She waved her arms furiously upward trying to catch the male farmer's attention. He smiled at her ... [foolishness] and gave her yet more directions. Arriving at her destination the reliable government sedan seemed to be swerving – Oh God, she thought, I have a flat tyre. Anxiety rose. She attempted to fight back feelings of inadequacy. She must now interview a woman a similar age to herself who works on the local council, runs a farm and has a child. The interview proceeds and the woman generously tells her story. In this space, the woman's home, she feels awkward but must present as knowledgeable and confident. She feels the difference in their lives, not simply difference about urban or rural lifestyle, but also difference around privilege. She is paid well and lives in a home, the woman lives in a shed. One room is where the family eats and sleeps. There is no bathroom in sight. The time came to leave. How to tell the women the tyre is flat and she can't change it? She feebly says, "I am not used to this type of car and can't change the tyre." The woman hands her the screaming child. She holds it at arm's length not knowing how to quieten it, not knowing how to hold it. The woman proceeds to change the tyre and pacify the child. She feels inadequate as a woman. (Bryant and Livholts, 2007:34–35) (Figure 14.3)

In the memory above, I recall feelings of vulnerability and the vastness of the countryside. I feel my body diminished and exposed. I feel "out of place" and stripped of competence (Bryant and Livholts, 2015:169). I am being forced to acknowledge my gendered and classed academic body and the gendered norms that I am unable to fulfil.

Figure 14.3 Driveway (Lia Bryant).

Being "in place" in this memory brings forth how we see rural places from our situated knowledges (Haraway, 1998). For me, being in place is a reflexive confrontation with my situated knowledge as a feminist academic shaped by multiple discourses and practices of gender (Bryant and Pini, 2011:142). Moral judgments also come into place. While these may come to the fore over the phone, in this instant it is the experience of the visuality of place, the moral middle-class judgment of where the woman lives and the sensory and embodied response to how to quieten a crying baby (Bryant and Livholts, 2015). What I understood through abstract knowledge became an experiential lesson – my moral judgments shaped my emotional, cognitive, and sensory responses to feeling out of place.

Looking back at this memory of myself as a younger woman in my 20s, I also learn that the embodied gaze of the woman I interviewed is missing. I wonder what her experience of my visiting was like? Did I disrupt, reinforce, or in any way shape her sense of place and gender? For me this story highlights the subtleties of place and the nuanced interactions that occur in place that for a rural researcher cannot be simply replaced by technologies during the pandemic.

In and put of place: virtual access

Here I am, 32 years later, at a time most of us could not have imagined. As a rural researcher, I have taken for granted that I can get into a car and a few hours later be in the country. I have taken for granted that I have access to being in place to experience and be challenged. Simply put, to feel place. It is important to me to shape my praxis through attempting to understand the people I research with, the communities I collaborate with and, in and out of this context, to attempt to understand myself. Recently, I had a telephone interview with a male farmer about co-designing resources for the prevention of male farmer suicide. I have been working on this topic for some years and I advocate for a place-based approach to tailoring suicide prevention that is community driven and state supported. I now need to undertake this research by phone. Hence, place in this context is restricted to voice, however, like face-to-face interactions, the farmer's expertise of distress, stories of assistance, and recovery in place are at the centre of the research which reinforce a place-based understanding.

I have always liked the rhythm and the nonsensical feeling to the word discombobulate. In the first instance, telephone-based research discombobulates me. At the time, I write:

> She got the time wrong. Of course there is a time difference across the states in Australia. She knows this. She rings people all the time in other states. But today she rings at the appointed 1 pm. 1 pm in New South Wales not her home town. She receives an email, "hey Lia did we get mixed up with our time zones? … I am available at 4 if you can ring." The farmer is so gracious.

Time is disrupted through the virtual, especially crossing time zones. But as I have been arguing, so are other things. I learn from the virtual some important lessons. The first, and most obvious – check the time in places other than your own! Secondly, a telephone interview requires me to listen differently. I am transfixed, I hold the phone tight as though this might bring me closer to where he is. I only have the voice in which to determine how he is feeling, how interested he is in the topic, how to build a relationship with him and put him at ease. I have to think about how I would hear gendered cues, how I would hear if a farming man is comfortable talking to me about male farmer suicide. Thirdly, and most importantly, will the phone make this easier or harder for him to communicate his emotions, experiences, and ideas?

Sarah Ahmed's (2004) argument that voices suppress and express emotions reshapes the way I hear. I attempt to determine what is being suppressed as well as expressed. I hear the pauses in how he speaks. The pauses I feel deep in my body. I think he pauses to garner space, to tentatively consider what is to be said next and how to express his emotions.

Literature focused on the telephone suggests that one of the first questions people ask when calling mobile phones is "Where are you?" (Garcia-Montes et al., 2006). It is interesting how we wish to place people. However, a phone conversation is anything but "unlocated" and people may be in multiple spaces within place as conversations unfold. As Bryant and Livholts (2013:12) suggest:

> when receiving and making telephone calls in the home it cannot be assumed that the individual is in one physical space during the course of the conversation … nor can it be assumed that there is one cognitive space as there is the possibility that the person is distracted, multitasking or indeed even having more than one conversation at the same time.

Despite COVID-19 restricting public movements, it is movements that happen in private spaces during moments of a telephone interview that cannot really be known. Face-to-face (and Zoom) interviews, more often than not, fix people in place. During this time of restriction, perhaps there is more to be known about how farming women and men move through private spaces and how this may shape how they narrate their lives and express emotions during telephone interviews.

In conclusion

I am suggesting a sensory engagement with place provides a stream of memories. It also enables a reflexive engagement with places and spaces which enables rural researchers to learn about the texture and complexity of how gendering occurs in time and place. It provides us with a location in which to examine how farmers negotiate social relations and our situatedness that disrupts time and place as we enter the rural. COVID restrictions alter our reflexive learning about place.

For now, I think of the yellow fields of wheat and wonder how long it will be until I see them flickering past once again. I look out the window of my own home. Paved garden, trimmed roses. While I am away from the rural by necessity, I try hard to remain engaged virtually with both places and people.

References

Ahmed, S. (2004) Declarations of Whiteness: The Non-performativity of Antiracism, *Borderlands e-journal*, 3, 2. Available from: http://www.borderlands.net.au/vol3no2_2004/ahmed_declarations.htm

Barad, K. (2003) Posthumanist Performativity: Toward an Understanding of How Matter Comes to Matter, *Signs: Journal of Women in Culture and Society*, 28, 3, 801–831.

Bryant, L. and George, J. (2016) *Water and Rural Communities*. Oxon: Routledge.

Bryant, L. and Livholts, M. (2007) Exploring the Gendering of Space by Using Memory Work as a Reflexive Research Method, *International Journal of Qualitative Methods*, 6, 29–43.

Bryant, L. and Livholts, M. (2013) Location and Unlocation: Examining Gender and Telephony Through Autoethnographic Textual and Visual Methods, *International Journal of Qualitative Methods*, 12, 1, 403–419.

Bryant, L. and Livholts, M. (2015) Memory Work and Reflexive Gendered Bodies: Examining Rural Landscapes in the Making, in eds Pini, B., Brandth, B. and Little, J., *Rural Feminisms*, Lanham: Lexington Books, 181–194.

Bryant, L. and Pini, B. (2011) *Gender and Rurality*, NY and UK, Routledge.

Butler, J. (1993) *Bodies that Matter: On the Discursive Limits of "Sex"*. New York: Routledge.

Garcia-Montes, J.M., Caballero-Munõ, S.D. and Pérez-Álvarez, M. (2006) Changes in the Self Resulting from the Use of Mobile Phones, *Media, Culture & Society*, 28, 1, 67–82.

Haraway, D. (1988) Situated Knowledges: The Science Question in Feminism and the Privilege of Partial Perspective, *Feminist Studies*, 14, 3, 575–599.

Haraway, D.J. (2008) *When Species Meet*. Minneapolis: University of Minnesota Press.

Jacobs, M. (2006) A Geography of Big Things, *Cultural Geographies*, 13, 1, 1–27.

Stewart, K. (2011) Atmospheric Attunements, Environment and Planning D: Society and Space, 29, 445–453.

Tolia-Kelly, D.P. (2011) The Geographies of Cultural Geography III: Material Geographies, Vibrant Matters and Risking Surface Geographies, *Progress in Human Geography*, 37, 1, 153–160.

15 Beyond COVID-19: building the resilience of vulnerable communities in African food systems

Lilian Nkengla-Asi, Marc J. Cohen, and María del Rosario Castro Bernardini

Introduction

The coronavirus pandemic lays bare the inequality and inefficiencies that pervade current food systems. Paradoxically, the very people who grow, process, package, and distribute food are being left behind, particularly women, youth, indigenous people, and immigrants.

This chapter offers a preliminary assessment of gendered impacts of COVID-19 on global food systems, hunger, and resilience. It focuses on the effects of the pandemic on smallholder farmers, particularly women, and examines inclusive policy options that foster progress toward zero hunger, climate-resilience, and gender equality by 2030.

The chapter centers on sub-Saharan Africa (SSA), as the region faced severe food-security challenges even before COVID-19. Its population living with hunger rose by 16 per cent between 2015 and 2019, reaching 234.7 million people, accounting for more than one of every three food-insecure people on earth. At 22 percent, SSA's food insecurity was substantially higher than the global figure of 8.9 percent (FAO et al., 2020). The prevalence of both moderate and severe food insecurity is significantly higher for African women than for the continent's men (FAO et al., 2020). Gender inequality in food insecurity stems from formal and informal discrimination that women and girls face in societies at large and within their households, in Africa and elsewhere (Botreau and Cohen, 2020). The pandemic has significantly exacerbated SSA's gender unequal food insecurity.

COVID-19's impact on food systems

COVID-19 has caused major disruptions in economic activities across the world, including SSA. The World Bank (2021) has estimated that economic

DOI: 10.4324/9781003198277-19

growth across the region declined from 2.4 percent in 2019 to 3.7 percent in 2020. This would be SSA's first recession in a quarter century, with major impacts on poverty and food insecurity. COVID-induced economic and social disruption has led to rising food prices, jeopardizing food access, availability, and affordability.

The pandemic has serious negative effects on food security in Southern and Western Africa in particular (Oxfam, 2020a, 2020b), interacting with other pre-existing crises such as climate change, locust disasters, and violence to create profound negative synergies. In East Africa, the food systems were already under strain pre-COVID-19. The population now faces a "triple menace" as heavy floods make it difficult to contain the locusts and the pandemic (cited in UN, 2020). With limited mobility and decreased consumers' purchasing power, food producers, workers, and market vendors lose opportunities to earn a viable income and supply food within and beyond their communities. Farmers have limited ability to access resources, plant, harvest, and sell their goods. Consequently, in early 2021, a spike in global hunger appears to be imminent as people are forced to make difficult decisions on how to use increasingly limited resources.

Furthermore, workers in the informal economy – including women, youth, and migrants – are particularly vulnerable. A rapid survey of businesses in Uganda suggests that lockdown measures reduced business activity by more than half and finds that micro- and small enterprises experienced a larger decline in activity compared to medium and large enterprises (Lakuma et al., 2020). Similarly, real-time survey data from Senegal, Mali, and Burkina Faso suggest that on average, by the end of April 2020, one out of four workers lost their jobs and one out of two workers experienced a decline in earnings. Informal sector workers are at higher risk, as they generally rely on daily sales for their earnings, lack mechanisms for collective bargaining, and tend to be in intensive activities (Balde et al., 2020).

Oxfam's partner in Zimbabwe, Knowledge Transfer Africa (KTA), using technology to provide market information on farm produce, reported that the threat of temporary closure of Mbare Musika market in Harare triggered panic buying and price increases of 257 percent for a head of cabbage and 33 percent each for 20 kg of sugar beans and a bucket of maize, the main staple (Dhewa, 2020). COVID-19-induced price increases put basic food stuffs beyond the reach of many urban people whose income streams have been strained by the lockdown (Oxfam, 2020a).

Exacerbating gender inequality

COVID-19 is much more than a health crisis. It has exacerbated gender inequality as women, particularly those from marginalized ethnic groups and communities, feel the consequences most acutely. Before the pandemic, around 50 percent of employed women in sub-Saharan Africa derived their income from agriculture (FAO, 2011) and faced challenges due to disempowering social norms (Berkhout et al., 2021). A higher percentage of women workers in SSA are concentrated in insecure informal sector employment, with less access to social protection; 92 percent, as compared to 86 percent of men workers. Outside of agriculture, the gender gap in informal employment is even larger; 83 percent of women workers compared to 72 percent of men (Bonnet et al., 2019). Likewise, a survey of pandemic-related business closures in three SSA countries (Ghana, Kenya, and Nigeria) found that women-owned businesses closed at a higher rate than those owned by men (Figure 15.1). COVID-19 also affects women and girls by adding to their care responsibilities.

Women play a pivotal role in ensuring household food security. Women and girls are at greater risk of experiencing negative impacts in contexts of crises due to existing gender discrimination and find themselves excluded from high-level policy debates and mitigation efforts (Botreau and Cohen, 2020; Berkhout et al., 2021). Rising poverty and hunger, along with lack of access to essential services in rural areas (De la O Campos et al., 2018), put women and girls at greater risk during crises. Without gender-responsive interventions, women and girls in rural areas face low access to knowledge, services, and technologies, limiting their access to COVID-19 information and creating challenges to follow protection measures

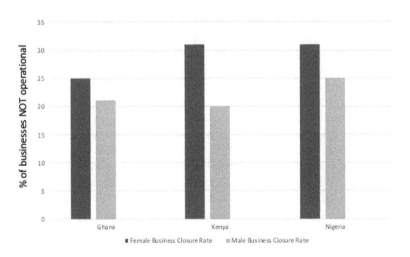

Figure 15.1 Business closure gender gap in Ghana, Kenya, and Nigeria (IDA, 2020).

such as hand-washing, staying at home, and maintaining social distance (Quisumbing et al., 2020).

Food security and agriculture-related policies and practices are often gender-blind or biased, limiting women's access to critical resources such as land, seeds, markets, finance, extension services, farm labor, climate information, and decision-making processes (Botreau and Cohen, 2020; FAO, 2020). Initial assessments of gender-related impacts of COVID-19 emphasized the economic effects of the pandemic on rural women's assets and livelihoods. Evidence from Bangladesh and Uganda shows that women's assets are usually sold first in a crisis, and that when a family member dies, inheritance practices often exclude women (Quisumbing et al., 2020). Bone, a 43-year-old petty trader and mother of eight children in Liberia, lost her job. Like many other Liberian women, she is her family's sole earner and also responsible for caring for her children and extended family. Bone told Oxfam, "I and my children ate two meals a day prior to COVID but now, it is either one meal a day or none" (Johnson-Mbayo K. B., 2020). COVID-19 is likely to exacerbate these challenges, leaving women farmers and traders less able to cope with shocks from crises.

Women around the world experience the burden of unpaid care and domestic work (CARE, 2020; Oxfam, 2021). Women workers find it challenging to integrate their work responsibilities with added care and domestic responsibilities in the context of school closures and mobility restrictions. When mothers need to leave the house to work during the pandemic, it typically falls on girls to take on unpaid care and domestic work (FAO, 2020). An interview with women refugees in Bria in the Central African Republic revealed that women often had increased responsibilities to care for children, the sick, and elderly, further exposing them to COVID-19. One displaced woman said, "It is often women who wake up early to take care of the home, go fetch water, and go to the market. Women are exposed and very vulnerable." The vice chair of the community protection structure added, "It is women who support their families with the small amount of money they have saved" (Oxfam, 2021).

Violence against women and girls rapidly increased in the wake of restrictions and lockdowns as families witnessed increased stress caused by losses of jobs, income, and food security. According to UN Women (2020), 243 million women and girls reported experiencing sexual and intimate partner violence during the pandemic. A study in Southern African Development Community member states indicates that in the first week of lockdown GBV increased as families spent more time at home together (Amnesty International, 2021). The South African Police Service (SAPS) reported receiving over 2,300 calls for help related to gender-based violence during the first week of lockdown (Amnesty International, 2021). Similarly, in Zimbabwe, local NGOs witnessed a spike in domestic violence during the first week of April (Amnesty International, 2021). Although conclusive data is not available, COVID-19-related conflicts and tensions could be exacerbating the risk of domestic and gender-based violence for rural households (FAO, 2020).

COVID-19 disproportionately impacts girls' education across Africa. School closures have led to increased unwanted pregnancies and early marriages. A rapid assessment conducted by the South African government found that almost 13,000 under-aged girls got pregnant and about 40,000 got married during a five-month school shutdown (Chisanje, 2021). One girl in Malawi who had completed primary school was looking forward to secondary when COVID-19 started. After COVID-19 struck, she had to stay home for five months due to school closure. During the break, her father married her off to an older man in a nearby village. "I am so devasted that I won't be able to attend secondary school because of what my father is forcing me to do," she said.

Policy issues for inclusive and gender-responsive food systems in Africa

African governments recognize the importance of gender-responsive agriculture and sustainable development particularly during crises. COVID-19 caused a scramble among governments to boost health and immediate COVID-19 response measures, meaning greater pressure on resources available for investment in sustainable agriculture and food security (Maeresera and Chikowore, 2020). COVID-19 revealed the fragility of health infrastructure and absence of social safety nets in many SSA countries which particularly affects women and the vulnerable. The pandemic offers a unique opportunity to reflect on what is needed to develop a food system that is gender-transformative, resilient, and sustainable. Such a system would ensure that the changes we make now will enable communities to better prepare for and respond to future shocks.

African Union (AU) member states agreed in 2003 to devote a minimum of 10 percent of their budgets to agriculture and reiterated this pledge for inclusive and sustainable agricultural development in the 2014 Malabo Declaration. Out of 49 member states reporting on the Malabo commitments during 2017 and 2018, just four were on track, and only Uganda made progress on achieving zero hunger by 2025 (AU, 2020). Moreover, the quantitative pledge of 10 percent of public expenditures to agriculture does not include specific targets to address the needs and aspirations of women and men smallholder farmers.

For their part, aid donors have underinvested in agriculture and rural development. Data from FAO and OECD indicate that in 2018, donors provided US$7.5 billion to the sector (in constant prices), accounting for less than 4 percent of all aid disbursements. Africa received the largest share of aid to agriculture of any global region, 39 percent. Two-thirds of all global aid disbursements to agriculture had gender equality as either its main purpose or a significant consideration.

Conclusion and policy recommendations

Governments in Africa should focus their agricultural development spending on women and men smallholder farmers. Sustainable, climate-resilient approaches should target women farmers, particularly their access to productive resources and services. Beyond increasing expenditures, governments and donors should create an enabling environment for women to exercise their rights and engage in active citizenship on policies that affect them.

Policymakers need to put gender justice at the core of policies aimed at addressing social inequalities and COVID-19's impacts (Hidrobo et al., 2020; CARE, 2020). Women must be represented in leadership in the design and implementation of social protection measures, welfare systems, and policies; collection and analyses of sex-disaggregated data are fundamental for gender-related impact assessment of crises and evidence-based formulation of policies to advance gender justice in rural areas (Feed the Future, 2020; Botreau and Cohen, 2020).

Governments should ensure that grassroots groups and women's rights organizations participate in budget decision-making. An example is the effort by the Economic Community of West African States (ECOWAS) network of parliamentarians for gender equality and investment in agriculture and food security coordinated by FAO, the International Institute for Sustainable Development (IISD), and Oxfam. It has played a key role during COVID-19 by creating awareness and sensitizing governments through webinars on the urgent need for inclusive and gender-equitable agricultural investment. It brought together parliamentarians from Africa, Europe, Latin America, and the Caribbean to reflect on their role in tackling the crisis to address rural women's needs and priorities on food security and nutrition (IISD, 2020).

Governments should adopt policies and regulations that promote good agricultural practices and benefit vulnerable people. Governments should provide incentives such as lifting value-added taxes, and duties imposed on food businesses to enable the smooth functioning of supply chains.

Government authorities should work with food companies, retailers, and private sector actors for an inclusive, transparent, and sustainable supply chain. Ghana's government has rolled out the Corona Virus Alleviation Program (CAP) to address economic, social, and health challenges that has provided food to 400,000 individuals in the areas affected by restrictions (Danquah et al., 2020). In a recent declaration, African Ministers of Agriculture committed to ensuring that measures are in place during the pandemic to support food security and nutrition for all (Trust Africa et al., 2020).

Ultimately, COVID-19 has brought to light the need for profound systemic transformation that includes recognition of the value of unpaid and underpaid care work, mainly supported by women and girls; the implementation of universally accessible social protection programs (Berkhout et al., 2021); and intensified gender-inclusive efforts to achieve equitable food systems.

References

Amnesty International (2021) *Treated like furniture: Gender-based violence response in Southern Africa*. London, UK: Peter Benenson House.

AU (African Union) (2020) *Second biennial review report of the AU Commission on the implementation of the Malabo Declaration on Accelerated Agricultural Growth and transformation for Shared Prosperity and Improved Livelihoods.* Addis Ababa: AU.

Balde, R., Boly, M., & Avenyo, E. (2020) 'Labour market effects of COVID-19 in Sub Saharan Africa: An informality lens from Burkino Faso, Mali, and Senegal'. Working Paper Series, Maastricht Economic and Social Research Institute on Innovation and Technology (UNU-MERIT).

Berkhout, E., Galasso, N., Lawson, M., Rivero Morales, P.A., Taneja, A., & Vázquez Pimentel, D.A. (2021) *The inequality virus: Bringing together a world torn apart by coronavirus through a fair, just, and sustainable economy.* Oxfam International.

Bonnet, F., Vanek, H., & Chen, M. (2019) *Women and men in the informal economy: A statistical brief.* Manchester, UK: WIEGO.

Botreau, H. & Cohen, M.J. (2020) 'Gender inequality and food insecurity: A dozen years after the food price crisis, rural women still bear the brunt of poverty and hunger' in Cohen, M.J. (ed.) *Advances in Food Security and Sustainability,* Volume 5. Cambridge, MA: Academic Press, pp. 53–117.

CARE (2020) *Building forward: Creating a more equitable, gender-just, inclusive, and sustainable world.* CARE International.

Chisanje, S. (2021) 'Safeguarding girls' education from COVID-19 ills', Oxfam in Southern Africa Told by Exposure (Covid-19 One Year Anniversary Opinion and Commentary Series), 24th February.

Danquah, M., Schotte, S., & Sen, K. (2020) 'COVID-19 and employment: Insights from the Sub-Saharan African experience'. *The Indian Journal of Labour Economics*, 63(1), pp. 23–30.

De La O Campos, A.P., Villani, C., Davis, B., & Takagi, M. (2018) *Ending extreme poverty in rural areas: Sustaining livelihoods to leave no one behind.* Rome: FAO.

Dhewa, C. (2020) 'Guest Column – The Musika COVID-19 dilemma: Closing markets will save lives, but it will also ruin them'. *newZWire*, 27 March.

FAO (Food and Agriculture Organization of the United Nations) (2011) *The state of food and agriculture: Closing the gender gap for development.* Rome: FAO.

FAO (2020) *Gendered impacts of COVID-19 and equitable policy responses in agriculture, food security, and nutrition.* Rome: FAO.

FAO, IFAD, UNICEF, WFP, & WHO (2020) *The State of food security and nutrition in the world 2020: Transforming food systems for affordable healthy diets.* Rome: FAO.

Feed the Future (2020) 'Gender responsive policy systems for inclusive and effective COVID-19 response'. *Agrilinks*, 12 August.

Hidrobo, M., Kumar, N., Palermo, T., Peterman, A., & Roy, S. (2020) 'Gender-sensitive social protection: A critical component of the COVID-19 response in low- and middle-income countries', *IFPRI Issue Brief 2020*. Washington, DC: IFPRI.

IDA (International Development Association, World Bank) (2020) *Responding to the emerging food security crisis.* Washington, DC: IDA.

IISD (International Institute for Sustainable Development) (2020) 'Parliamentarians Action for Gender Equality and Food Security as a Response to COVID-19', Webinar, 17 June 2020.

Johnson-Mbayo, K.B. (2020) 'A family struck by hunger due to coronavirus'. Oxfam in West Africa.

Lakuma, P.C., Sunday, N., Sserunjogi, B., Kahunde, R., & Munyambonera, E.F. (2020) 'How has the COVID-19 pandemic impacted Ugandan businesses? Results from a business climate survey', Economic Policy Research Center, Special Issue No. 01.

Maeresera, E. & Chikowore, A. (2020) 'Will the Cure Bankrupt Us? Official development assistance and the COVID-19 response in Southern African countries', Oxfam & AFRODAD Joint Agency Briefing Note.

Oxfam (2020a) 'Coronavirus could increase hunger for over 40 million in Southern Africa', Oxfam International, 4th June.

Oxfam (2020b) 'COVID-19: 50 million people threatened by hunger in West Africa', Oxfam International, 21st April.

Oxfam (2020c) 'The Hunger Virus: How COVID is fueling hunger in a hungry world', Oxfam Media Briefing, 9th July.

Oxfam (2021) 'Effects of COVID-19 to women', Video, Oxfam Facebook, 15 March 2021.

Quisumbing, A., Kumar, N., Meinzen-Dick, R.S., & Ringler, C. (2020) 'Why gender matters in COVID-19 responses – now and in the future' in Swinnen, J

& McDermott, J. (eds.) *COVID-19 and global food security*. Washington, DC: IFPRI, pp. 88–90.

Trust Africa, CNC, ESAFF, & Oxfam (2020) 'The impact of COVID-19 on small-scale farming, food security, and sovereignty in Africa'. *AU Lobby Note*.

UN (United Nations) (2020) 'The impact of COVID-19 on food security'. *Policy Brief.*

UN Women (2020) 'The shadow pandemic: Violence against women and girls and COVID-19'.

World Bank (2021) *Global economic prospects, January 2021*. Washington, DC: World Bank.

Conclusion

As this book came to press, we hoped that the COVID-19 pandemic would be behind us but we see that around the world we still struggle to deal with the many ongoing consequences of the pandemic. Nevertheless, we have learned many lessons about gender, food, and agriculture during this difficult time.

First, relying on an industrial global system for food security is precarious in times of crisis. People who experienced food insecurity before the pandemic were most vulnerable when the pandemic hit. As in past disasters and episodes of food scarcity, hunger hit people not so much because no food was available, but because they could not afford to purchase food. When food insecurity increases in households, particularly in South Asia, but also in other parts of the world, women are the first and most likely to suffer deprivation.

As the pandemic progressed and countries imposed lockdowns, disrupted supply chains caused problems for farmers, farm workers, food processors, and consumers. Women small-scale farmers and fishers could not get their produce to market in Honduras, India, and Nepal. In other places, such as Vietnam, women farmers innovated their production and showed resiliency through social responsibility, informal networks, and a commitment to environmental sustainability.

Farmworkers, food processing workers, grocery store workers, and restaurant workers emerged as both essential and vulnerable. Some migrant farmworkers such as those in India lost their jobs during lockdowns. Others, and food processing workers, such as those in Iowa, continued to work, but experienced high-level exposure and illness from COVID-19 due to unsafe working and living conditions that prevented social distancing and safety practices during COVID-19.

Many national governments initiated programs to provide food, health, and support to farmers and fishers, but often had a minimum criteria of land size or formal registration that prevented women from receiving benefits, such as in Nepal and Bangladesh. In many parts of the world, women's groups and organizations stepped in to fill the gap by providing support and resources for rural women. In Honduras, Nepal, Kenya, and the United States, these groups quickly shifted to support people impacted severely by COVID-19 and lockdowns with food, clean water, masks, information, and social support.

Another example of the important role of collective action, the Black Lives Matter movement driven by the extreme injustices and police violence against BIPOC, coincided with some of the highest pandemic impacts. Despite the risk, many took to the streets, in the United States and in many other parts of the world, to voice their unrest. Carter's and Shervey's chapters illustrate the heavy importance of intersectionality in the food system and our understanding of injustices experienced by many women of color. Going forward, both research and activism will be needed to continue the fight for justice, especially for workers within our food system.

Across the globe, authors report a significant increase in women's unpaid care work. Much care work involves food including feeding families, friends, and communities. Once again, intersectional inequalities result in women, racial and ethnic minorities, migrants, and queer people experiencing the greatest increases in care work. The work of getting food and water for their families expanded, and the time required to do so increased. Feeding their families in times of higher food prices and less food security disproportionately fell on women's shoulders. Often family members needed to be fed at home and many lost access to meals previously provided at school or work.

Research

Researchers report stark differences between their own situation and that of the rural people they are studying. Researchers, regardless of country, often work from home in relative safety compared to vulnerable people who work on the front lines such as meat processing workers, market vendors, and farmworkers. These differences in vulnerabilities and safety raise ethical questions for researchers about conducting research in these difficult times. Many researchers report not being able to travel to the places they usually do research such as rural Australia, Indonesia, Alaska, Honduras and other places, keeping them far removed from the communities they study. But for many, research does continue with local partners or through phone calls or emails. Access to the Internet and mobile phones remains a highly gendered issue, especially in rural and remote locations, thus making research and hearing and representing the voices of the most marginalized people even more difficult. The authors of chapters on Vietnam, Nepal, Honduras, and other places show how collaborating with local partners allows research on gender, agriculture, and food to continue in rural locations.

Future research topics

The experiences reported in this book suggest many topics for future research including the continued insistence on sex- and gender-disaggregated data collection and analysis and beyond. We need expanded work on the forms and precarity of women's labor under a variety of circumstances, including emergency and disaster conditions. We need more research on the ubiquity of women's care work and its many manifestations in the home, the community, and the labor market. Much of this work is hidden or taken for granted. The mental labor embedded in care forms a prime example, making the relationship between gender and mental forms of domestic labor a pressing topic. The physical labor that goes into care work is only one component of the effort involved, but must be expanded to include the substantial time and stress of the accompanying mental labor. For example, feeding a household requires much planning in food acquisition, preparation, and distribution, made more difficult when easy access to food sources is limited or eliminated. Virtually every component of food provision and agriculture entails mental labor overlooked until revealed by challenges such as the pandemic. Suddenly, simple decisions become weighty issues of health and safety for you and your loved ones.

Another topic for more research is care work at the community level. Women's family and household care work are recognized if not sufficiently valued compared to the less well known work they perform for the larger community. It became very obvious during COVID-19, that survival often requires community-level collective action, and this book documents important examples. Understanding the forms, circumstances, and benefits that ensue adds an important item to the research agenda. The value of collective action more generally is uncovered by these stories of hope and suggests another avenue for future research.

Other topics include more research on masculinities, men's roles in care work, and influences on the gendered division of labor in its provision. While COVID-19 has highlighted the disproportionate burdens of care experienced by women, many men have also had to step up their efforts in balancing responsibilities. How has the gendered division of labor on care work changed, in what ways, and under what circumstances? What happens in families and households with different gender roles and compositions? Similarly, research on care work within diverse gender and sexuality identities and communities and any alternative models for its provision needs to be ramped up.

Most of the reports in this book illustrate the struggles and challenges women faced. However, there are also examples, such as in Vietnam, where some women entrepreneurs prospered during the pandemic, bolstered by a combination of entrepreneurship and fortuitous circumstances. Can research show the ways that success stories can be built upon and replicated?

Finally, these accounts underscore how much more needs to be done to fully realize gender-transformative research questions and methods. This may require research on research methods themselves. What works best to foster collaborative, participatory, and inclusive research programs? How can research be supported in times of disruption such as the pandemic, especially when most funding mechanisms are built on old hierarchical models? How can intersectional approaches be systematically and contextually sensitively applied, and how can ethical concerns with power differentials be reconciled with the requirements of researchers, funders, and participants who may have different agendas?

Future policy directions

Many of the policy recommendations that emerge from these accounts are not specific to the pandemic but rather are given new urgency by its ravages; for example, recognizing that care work is work and deserves both financial and moral support, regardless of who delivers it is critical. Strong safety net and social welfare policies can help cushion the burdens and impacts that are documented here. In the United States, the dismantling of the safety net over the last several decades, the lack of strong support for child and elder care, the failure to raise the minimum wage to a living wage, and huge racial, ethnic, and class disparities in access to health care and in precarious employment combined to exacerbate pandemic impacts. Places with these types of programs assist their populations to manage during extreme circumstances. And the converse is devastating. Poor nations with few social supports are unable to provide relief to their populations. In all cases, new policy must recognize invisible populations, work, and other activities that too often fall below the radar of official statistics and programs. COVID has underscored that around the world the extent to which the huge and growing disparities in resources, including wealth, income, and health, as they intersect with gender create need and demand new policy to address these issues.

This continues to be evident as vaccine development and distributions are unevenly reaching the masses. Within the United States, while rollout has ramped up incredibly, there are still differences in how vaccines are reaching communities, including the elderly, high-risk groups, rural communities, and communities of color. There are also gender differences in who is receiving vaccines and who is not signing up. Globally, extreme differences exist in vaccine availability, with many countries in the Global South unable to access and implement any widespread distribution, while facing major spikes in cases and hospitalizations. We need a global concerted and cooperative effort to manage these increases in cases, to prevent more variants from developing and spreading, and to return to any normalcy for everyone.

Beyond the need for stronger, more equitable, and gender-sensitive social welfare and health care policies and programs are specific policies for food and agriculture workers and sectors. These workers are often the most poorly paid, with the fewest resources to fall back on in difficult times. In many places, women are unpaid family labor with little access or rights to either land or wages on their own. In other areas, many are undocumented, informal, or otherwise unrecognized workers. Organizing for better working conditions and support has seen an upsurge during COVID-19, but it's not yet clear to what effect. In general, policies to recognize, regularize, and improve working conditions and compensation for all food and agricultural workers, but especially women and other marginalized workers, are necessary steps exposed by the pandemic.

The need for strong local food systems also became obvious during the pandemic. As supply chains broke down and shortages emerged in many places, the lack of supply and control hindered access to markets and food to the detriment of both producers and consumers. Farmers lost markets and access to customers. Consumers experienced lack of goods, often in the same locale. In between, the ravages of the disease on processing workers further exacerbated disruptions on supply. Support for more robust local systems, while not a panacea, would make the connections between producers, processors, and consumers less vulnerable to global crises.

Finally, the pandemic demonstrates the necessity for better access to communications and information technology. Although not specific to COVID-19, the pandemic made the gaps and disparities more obvious and the need to rectify them more pressing. Broadband access should be universal across space and place and regardless of gender, race, ethnicity, class, age, or household composition. The fact that even the richest nations have big gaps in coverage that adversely affect large swathes of their populations makes the issue relevant on a global scale.

Translating policy into gender-transformative programs will not be easy. However, the pandemic also demonstrates what collective action, both formal and informal and at different scales, can accomplish. Accounts of community-based networks and organizations to provide goods, services, and care provide hope as they are both inspirational and aspirational as models of resilience. The pandemic has exacerbated existing inequalities, highlighting points of unequal access to resources, distribution of many responsibilities within the household and in our communities, as well as many discriminatory practices embedded within health care, employment, and justice systems, impacting our food system. While the impact of the pandemic has been and continues to be devastating, it presents an opportunity – an opportunity to collectively address these inequities and make real change. The question remains: will we come together and make progress related to gender and agriculture, or will we return to the status quo? The production of effective vaccinations in little more than a year is an amazing accomplishment of science and technology harnessed to a social good that provides new hope for when we emerge from the ravages of the pandemic. We look forward to similar effort in addressing the pressing issues of gender equality and transformation to bring food justice to all.

Index

Page numbers in *italics* represent the location of figures or photographs

www.ingramcontent.com/pod-product-compliance
Ingram Content Group UK Ltd.
Pitfield, Milton Keynes, MK11 3LW, UK
UKHW020414010325
455677UK00029B/886